Learn more @ www.askdessa.com

Dessa Kaspardlov

THE FIREMAN & THE WAITRESS

The *Dessanomics*™ Way to
Unlock Your Wealth Potential

Dessa Kaspardlov
Visit my website at www.askdessa.com

Printed in Canada

Originally printed under ISBN 978-0-9813040-0-7 in July 2009

Library and Archives Canada Cataloguing in Publication

Kaspardlov, Dessa
    The fireman and the waitress / Dessa Kaspardlov.

ISBN 978-1-77069-353-1

    1. Finance, Personal. I. Title.

HG179.K3755 2011   332.024   C2011-905062-5

This book is dedicated to my father, Dr. Melvin Kaspardlov (1923-1995), who always told me two things:

1. Don't waste time or money.
2. Every man can be wealthy, he just needs the right navigator.

Thanks, Dad. I put the two together.

To my clients and my readers. Thank you for sharing your stories, and thank you for allowing me to be a part of your success. You inspire me and our team at KL&A to grow and learn – every day.

To my family and friends. Thanks for your love and support over the years and especially during the writing of this book.

Thank you, Dessa.

ACKNOWLEDGEMENTS

∎ ∎ ∎

Lori Bamber

The HCA Group

Bruce McDougall

DESSANOMICS™

■ ■ ■

T he "too-good-to-be-true" truth that can make a million dollar difference by doing things differently.

Dessanomics is an innovative, revolutionary approach that will enable you to increase your personal wealth and pay off your debt. It teaches you the difference between good debt and bad debt, and how to capitalize on the good while getting rid of the bad. It's not a crazy theory based on impractical "diet" budgets and cutting out your daily cup of coffee. It's about restructuring your cash flow, paying yourself first and guaranteeing a predictable, sustainable future.

The concept of "pay yourself first" has been drilled into us by our financial advisors, parents and friends. They tell us to do it, but they don't tell us HOW to do it. The common sense, realistic methods found in *Dessanomics* will show you how to move yourself to the front of the "pay line," thereby guaranteeing an efficient cash flow. Efficient cash flow is king and it's the key that we've been missing for years.

Keep your money, grow your money, save for retirement and pay off your debt – all while continuing to live your life – that's the truth of *Dessanomics*.

CONTENTS

■ ■ ■

Foreword xvii

Introduction xxi

[1] MEET THE YOUNGS 01

The Starting Point:
Another Day Older and Deeper In Debt 03

The Payoff 11

[2] UNDERSTANDING DEBT 15

DESSANOMICS KEY #1. When you incur debt to
gain wealth (as with a mortgage), that's a good thing. 15

DESSANOMICS KEY #2. When you incur debt to
gain wealth AND get a tax refund, that's a really good
thing. Borrowing to invest, commonly known as
leveraging, is an example. 16

DESSANOMICS KEY #3. When you incur debt just
because you want a really special bottle of wine for your
anniversary dinner, or for any purpose other than building
wealth, that's a bad thing. 16

DESSANOMICS KEY #4. Never, ever pay off the
good debt first. 18

Ending the Balance Sheet Two-Step 19

Assets Minus Liabilities = Net Worth (A-L=NW) 22

DESSANOMICS KEY #5. Clean up your balance sheet
to pay as little as possible in interest and taxes: debt in one
account and savings in the other equal higher interest to
your banker, higher taxes for your government, and less
wealth for you! 27

DESSANOMICS **KEY #6.** When you pay less to banks and government, you free up cash flow. When you free up cash flow, you increase your ability to build wealth. 27

[3] GOING WITH THE (CASH) FLOW 29

Goodbye High Interest – Hello All-In-One HELOC! 30

The Downside of Diversification 34

DESSANOMICS **KEY #7.** Diversified investments are great. Diversified debts are expensive and inefficient. An all-in-one home equity line of credit (HELOC) allows you to pay less interest and pay debts faster..........37

Thinking Like a Business 37

[4] EFFICIENT CASH IS KING 45

DESSANOMICS **KEY #8.** Many people try to "pay themselves first" when they're saving for retirement, but really, they're standing third in line behind their lenders and the taxman. *Dessanomics* is the only system that puts you at the front of the line! 51

[5] ENSURING YOUR SINGLE GREATEST ASSET – YOUR EARNING POWER 53

Quality of Life Insurance............................59

DESSANOMICS **KEY #9.** An experienced advisor can help you buy the right kind of insurance for you, in the right amount, at the right price. You deserve the peace of mind and security, and so does your family. 63

[6] YES, MOLLY, YOU NEED TO INVEST IN THE STOCK MARKET, EVEN IN RETIREMENT, BUT YOU DON'T HAVE TO LOSE SLEEP 65

Longer Lives, Smaller Dollars 67

DESSANOMICS **KEY #10.** In order to outpace inflation, you need to include equities in your retirement plan, but you don't have to put your savings at risk. With guarantees, you can buy affordable insurance protection for your greatest asset – your future. ..70

Mutual Funds Versus Segregated Funds 71

GMWB: Your New BFF 75

[7] PUTTING IT ALL TOGETHER
– DESSANOMICS IN ACTION 79

[8] WORKING THE PLAN 85

[9] RETIRING THE MORTGAGE 99

The Retirement Purse 104

Weighing the Risks 107

DESSANOMICS **KEY #11.** The risks of not using leverage can be far greater than the risks of using leverage. The key is to use conservative leverage in the context of a solid overall retirement plan. 110

[10] AFTERWORD – GETTING THE ADVICE
YOU NEED 111

DESSANOMICS **KEY #12.** Get the help you deserve to create an efficient retirement planning system. While this process can help anyone with income, it's essential that it be tailored to your individual needs. 114

DESSANOMICS WORKBOOK 117

DESSANOMICS **KEY #13.** To be healthy is something you value. To lose 10 lbs. is a goal. 117

FOREWORD

■ ■ ■

In more than 20 years of working with people and their money – after writing seven books, hundreds of magazine and newspaper articles and countless radio and TV editorials on the subject of personal finance – I rarely run into anything new.

I've interviewed myriad advisors and other financial experts over the years, and although I always enjoy talking to them, the terrain is terribly familiar.

But in the first 10 minutes I spent on the telephone with Dessa Kaspardlov, as I interviewed her for a special report I was writing for the Globe and Mail, I knew I'd discovered something completely unique and very exciting: something that had the capacity to make a real, significant and sustainable difference in people's lives.

As a former financial advisor, I understand the ability that advisors have to empower their clients' relationship with money. As coaches, advisors can help clients look into the future and make informed, effective decisions. They can help us clarify our vision of the future to the degree that we actually enjoy putting money aside for tomorrow that we could very easily spend today.

But what advisors can't do, and are often expected to do, is change the laws of investment.

Many people look to advisors to deliver the magic bullet that will rescue them from the real challenge they face: an inability to save enough money to meet their goals.

Life is expensive, and because we can't save enough, we want high investment returns to make up the difference. And we also want to be protected from loss, for while the idea of "risk" may be manageable, the reality of loss is not.

But the laws of risk and return cannot be repealed for more than a brief moment. We will forget again; for now, however, this latest downturn has reminded us that when those laws reinstate their force, the impact is dreadful.

Once again, too many Canadians found that they'd taken on more risk than they could afford. Why? Because once the financial plan was prepared, they realized they could not save enough to meet their financial goals. There are then only two choices: reduce retirement expectations or take on more risk in the portfolio.

But what if there were another way? Thanks to *Dessanomics*, there is.

Within these pages, Dessa demonstrates the strategies she has applied and refined over many years of helping clients build real and lasting wealth. By focusing first on paying debt efficiently and reducing the tax burden, she has created a means that will enable most middle-income families to do the formerly impossible: find enough disposable income to fulfill their retirement dreams without having to expose their nest egg to destructive market forces.

Dessa also understands something that many advisors choose to overlook: when people lose money, even if those losses are only on paper because they don't need the money today, it affects their quality of life. There really aren't many people who will work hard all their lives to save money and then sleep well at night when that money is exposed to the volatility of the stock markets. And while having a secure way to meet living expenses in retirement is essential for wellbeing, so is good health. Researchers have conclusively proven that stress is almost as bad for our long-term health as smoking, so to achieve a comfortable retirement, it is essential that our financial plans reduce our stress levels.

Does that sound like the experience of the average investor over the past two years?

That's why Dessa recommends investments that do exactly that – reduce stress. With insurance products that provide a guarantee against loss of principal and even a minimum guaranteed withdrawal amount, Canadians who apply *Dessanomics* can buy peace of mind and a secure future; as she describes it, your own private, guaranteed pension plan.

For too long, we've lived in a world in which only a small percentage of our population could look forward to the comfort and security of a guaranteed pension in retirement. (Yes, Canada's public retirement pension programs are terrific, but they replace only a small portion of our income.)

For the first time, we now have a strategy that allows every one of us to look forward to a secure retirement without sacrificing quality of life or peace of mind today.

It's about time.

Lori Bamber

A freelance writer, Lori Bamber is the author of seven books on personal finance and investment and an inspiring keynote speaker and workshop facilitator. Her articles appear regularly in special reports within the Globe & Mail and Report on Business, and Lori is widely quoted in publications such as Canadian Living and Today's Parent as a personal finance writer. She co-hosted CKNW's daily Moneyline, guest-hosted Money Talks on the Corus Radio Network, and has been a guest on Marketplace, The Gill Deacon Show and CBC Newsworld.

INTRODUCTION

■ ■ ■

At the age of 17, I took Harry Browne's "You Can Profit from a Monetary Crisis" (1974) from my father's personal library. My girlfriends were immersed in the latest issue of Seventeen Magazine; I was trying to understand if the U.S. economy (and that of the world) was coming to an end.

It did not, it has not and most likely will not. If you suspect I had no comprehension of what I was reading, you're right. To be perfectly frank, I'm not even sure if I ever finished the book. Over the years, however, I have finished reading so many books on finance I cannot count them. They are in my library today, along with all of my father's books.

I have learned to look far into the future for my clients. I have implemented many strategies that are useful, appropriate and work so very well for the wealthy.

But this book is not for the wealthy. It's for everyone else – people who have worked hard all their lives and who have done reasonably well, but will never spend more time worrying about their estate than about funding their retirement. It's about getting you to the point where you, too, can implement all of those strategies that you've read about.

When my soon-to-be husband, Dennis Laverty, decided to make a major career change so he could marry me and I could stay close to my children, he looked to the financial services industry. He believed, rightly, that it would close the deal: I would accept his proposal and get what I wanted, which was him and my children. Little did he know what was in store.

He learned very quickly that, in today's financial industry, the old method of attempting to squeeze blood out of a stone was virtually impossible. At one time, the industry trained us to keep lowering our price until a client finally made a commitment to buy. It did not matter what product we were trying to sell, the pitch went something like this: "Can you afford $100 each month for life insurance?" If the prospective client said no, we were trained to continue to hammer down the price until it was low enough.

The client would finally make a commitment, not because the price was finally low enough, but because it was 10 o'clock at night and he or she wanted us out of his or her kitchen. (Might I just say, in our minds, this COULD NOT be rewarding.)

Dennis and I learned we could not do business this way, so we set out to create a plan that would make it possible for our clients to achieve their goals.

In those days I had learned from experience that cash flow was king. You cannot get someone to pay for something when he doesn't have the cash flow to do so – and we couldn't offer a solution until the client understood that he or she had a problem.

We started by asking clients to provide us with their current financial information, including bank statements. From there, we looked for ways to reduce or eliminate interest cost and income tax, knowing that, in wealth creation or wealth preservation, those are the two primary wealth killers. In the process, we restructured cash flow so our clients could achieve their goals. By comparing our plan to what they were doing, we proved to them on paper (using charts and graphs) that our method was better. We did this simply by showing our clients how they could use the money they were sending to the bank and the government for their own benefit.

To our benefit, we no longer had to squeeze blood out of a stone. But something else also happened; not only did clients achieve a much better financial position by taking control, they also achieved peace of mind. They had truly taken control of their destiny, and they understood exactly what the best and worst-case scenario was.

You see, it isn't that Canadians don't understand they need to invest in their future and pay down their debt. They understand clearly that, if they deposit $1,000 to their RRSP, the government will repay them about $400. The problem is that they simply couldn't do that efficiently. Until now.

As time passed, our process evolved, as did the financial products in the marketplace. People in the industry got wind of what we were doing and wanted to learn more. Several years ago I presented my case study to a group of top Canadian financial advisors at a national conference.

I was nervous. Until that time, I had never done any public speaking. But Dennis knew I could do it, because I do the same thing day in and day out in client presentations.

When I got to the conclusion of my case and started showing the graphs, the audience of seasoned advisors all said "Wow!" (You will read about this case a little later.)

I knew then I had something that could benefit all Canadians, and now I want to share it with you.

Chapter 1:

MEET THE YOUNGS

■ ■ ■

The end of RRSP season was looming. As usual, Mel and Molly Young were feeling stressed about what to do with their annual contribution. And as usual, thinking about their RRSP contribution brought back all the anxiety they felt about being unprepared for retirement.

Unlike a lot of Canadians, they had managed to put aside $10,000 during the year. They felt good about the fact that they'd managed to save for a larger-than-average RRSP contribution. But now they weren't sure where to invest it.

Mel and Molly had worked with a financial advisor for some time. They'd never been completely satisfied with the relationship, partly because their friends Hank and Linda Lauzon always seemed to be doing so much better.

That's where I come in. I'm a financial advisor, and I had worked with Hank and Linda for many years. I was delighted when they referred Mel and Molly to me.

During our first telephone conversation, Mel explained that he and his wife had been friends of the Lauzons for most of their lives. They went to school together, were in each other's wedding parties, had children at about the same time and went on family vacations together. Mel and Hank worked at the same company and played in the same golf league in the summer.

"But lately," Mel said, "Hank and Linda seem to be getting way ahead of us financially. We can't figure it out, because Hank and I earn about the same income, and Linda doesn't work. They're never worried about making their RRSP contribution, they don't fight about money – ever – and Hank just bought a new Harley Davidson."

> It's hard to argue against increasing your net worth by using money that would otherwise go to the government or the bank.

Mel and Molly were in the same position as a lot of hard-working Canadians. They wanted to save for retirement and pay their debts off faster, but despite acting on the advice they had received, they were just not getting ahead as fast as they thought they should.

And although they didn't know it, they paid far more income tax and interest on their debts than they had to.

"I think I can help you," I said. "Without knowing much about your situation, I'm betting that you're paying more in income tax than you have to – certainly more than Hank and Linda, even though you're making roughly the same income. I am a firm believer that we must pay our fair share of income tax, but not a penny more."

As Mel and Molly were to find out, I've created a process for my clients, including Hank and Linda, that ensures they keep as much of it as possible in their pockets. I like to call it "*Dessanomics*™" – and as the Lauzons know from experience, it makes a real difference.

No other method generates the cash flow that will allow you to add more money to your investment portfolio and gain long-term wealth. If you're willing to change your lifestyle or get another job, *Dessanomics* will work even more efficiently!

THE STARTING POINT:
ANOTHER DAY OLDER AND DEEPER IN DEBT

Explaining that I would have to do a full analysis of their entire financial picture, I asked Mel for an overview of their current financial situation.

He and Molly were saving about $10,000 each year in an RRSP, and had saved a total of $140,000 for their retirement. (According to Statistics Canada, only 31% of the tax filers who were eligible to contribute to an RRSP in 2007 actually did it, and the median contribution was only $2,780.)

♟

- Mel and Molly made accelerated, bimonthly mortgage payments, and had increased their home's equity value by renovating.
- They had a savings account with about $20,000 put aside for the inevitable rainy day.
- Their two children, Jo Layne and Cori, were in university and would both graduate, debt-free, in the next few years.
- They both had term life insurance policies, but they were about to expire.

In other words, Mel and Molly were hard working, responsible citizens and parents who had done everything they were advised to do. But they felt a lot of financial anxiety, and they didn't feel they were making as much progress as they could.

They were right.

"I'm not sure what else we can do," said Mel, something I hear from almost every new client. "We are doing every single thing our financial advisor tells us to do. We're doing everything the experts in the papers and on TV tell us to do. But we just don't seem to be getting ahead. Sure, we could put away a few more dollars if we cut back on everything. But there is no way I am going to cut my annual golf trip to Myrtle Beach with the boys. And Molly will kill me if we don't go on our yearly cruise."

"Mel, I'm not going to tell you to give up your vacations," I replied. "But what if I told you that you could grow your wealth and pay down your mortgage faster, reduce your taxes, have a source of funds for that rainy day, and still go on vacation? Would you be interested?"

Mel didn't answer my question, but he asked one that had clearly been on his mind for a while. "Is that how Hank got the Harley?"

Of course, I could never disclose private information about my clients, but I was happy to reassure Mel that, with our process, his wealth would grow a lot faster.

There will undoubtedly be some naysayers who claim that *Dessanomics* isn't an effective strategy for paying off debt because borrowers are no longer chained to a traditional payment plan controlled by their lender. I say "bunk," because I've seen this plan work so elegantly and efficiently in the lives of my clients.

Two weeks later Mel and Molly arrived in my office for our initial meeting, with the information I'd asked them to bring. It included their income tax returns, household budget and copies of their investment, mortgage, loan and insurance statements.

Then they began to tell me their story. It may sound familiar to you. It certainly sounded familiar to me. Almost all my clients had a similar story when they first came to me.

Married over 25 years, Mel and Molly found themselves in the same situation as most boomers today, wondering how they were ever going to retire. They still had more than 15 years of payments on their house, not to mention the line of credit at the bank. They knew they had to invest more money for retirement to have the kind of lifestyle they wanted, but there just wasn't enough money to invest. They had counted on stock market performance to make up the difference, but with the latest declines, they realized that was unrealistic.

In addition, like a growing number of Canadians, Mel did not have a pension plan with his employer.

In my experience, even people lucky enough to have a pension worry that it won't be there when they need it. We've all heard about companies running into trouble and not being able to meet their pension obligations.

In particular, unless you work for the government, defined benefit plans, which provide a pre-determined monthly payment in retirement, are going the way of the dinosaur. As late as the mid-1980s, most major companies had defined benefit plans. Now, hardly one in ten companies has one.

That's a clear call to action. We need to create our own "Personal Pension Plan."

> When Patti and I first met Dessa about 10 years ago, we had some goals for retirement, the kids' education and dreams for a cottage and lots of travel. *Dessanomics* has helped us make sure those goals become reality. This process has enabled us to put everything in place so that even in this tough economy, we're still on track to retire as planned in 7-8 years. We traveled to Fiji for our anniversary, and you know that cottage we'd dreamed about? It's ours! *Dessanomics* works!
>
> **THE PRINTER & THE COMPUTER ANALYST**

Reducing your debt cost and income tax, and applying that cash flow to building your net worth, are the two most powerful wealth generators I know.

The Youngs knew they had to do everything in their power to save more, or they'd be in trouble in retirement. But they were also smart enough to know that, despite their best efforts, the numbers were not adding up.

Mel had been on the Internet, and he showed me his retirement projections. If he kept making his RRSP contributions and his accelerated mortgage payments, he could pay off the house in 15 years. He and Molly would be able to retire with about $675,000.

But $675,000 would produce an income of about $54,000 per year, assuming they withdrew 8% annually, which they knew was aggressive. That was only about a third of what they were living on, and they didn't feel their lifestyle was luxurious.

In fact, many experts recommend withdrawing no more than 4% or 5% from the retirement portfolio each year to ensure that your money lasts as long as you do. As I shared with Mel and Molly, this is a conundrum for many people who rely on their RRIFs, because Canada Revenue regulations state that about 8% must be withdrawn from the RRIF each year starting at age 72. If you live beyond age 95, your RRIF will become fully depleted.

Mel and Molly also worried about their mutual funds, and sometimes argued about whether they should be in the stock market at all. Their advisor had convinced them that equity investments do better over the long term and that only with stock market investments could they hope to outpace inflation and ensure their money lasted at least as long as they did. But after living through the technology market meltdown, they both worried about the effect of a big market correction. (And that was before we had the mother of all market corrections to worry about in the fall of 2008.)

"What if we lose 30% of our savings just before we retire? I don't have a pension, you know," Mel repeated.

At 49, Mel was a skilled tradesman who volunteered as a fireman in his spare time. His employment income was approximately $140,000 per year, but that included enormous amounts of overtime. Last year, his income had reached an all-time high of $170,000. But with the economy already showing signs of strain, Mel wasn't sure how long the overtime was going to last.

As a volunteer fireman, he earned an additional $10,000 each year. Mel had plenty of unused RRSP contribution room, over $60,000, and this year's contribution would barely make a dent. Rather than adding to their RRSP, he and Molly had been busy paying off their mortgage, which they saw as a guaranteed return investment. It's a very common strategy today, perhaps because we learned from our parents and grandparents that paying off the mortgage as quickly as possible was important.

But as I tell all my clients, things were different then. Grandpa had a guaranteed pension, he did not have a car loan, a line of credit, or credit card debt. They simply weren't available. (By the way, your eyes won't stay crossed if you make that face at your sister one too many times, either. Grandpa was just plain wrong about that one.)

Paying down your mortgage quickly is better than doing nothing at all. But I will tell you about another strategy that can help you pay off your mortgage faster while exponentially speeding up your wealth creation.

Molly was 45 when we first met. She worked part-time at the local greasy spoon, the only place in town that served Black Angus steak with eggs. Including her tips, she brought home about $30,000 each year. Beating the pension odds, Molly actually had a small Locked-In Retirement Account (LIRA) worth about $15,000, left over from a previous job as an accounts payable clerk.

When she was raising her children, working as a server gave Molly the flexibility she needed to be home with her kids when they needed her. Now that they were grown, Molly knew that some of her office skills were outdated. More importantly, she really enjoyed her job. She had no intention of going back to a nine-to-five office environment.

Mel and Molly bought their home several years before and still had an outstanding mortgage of $125,000. As Mel mentioned during our first conversation, they were making regular bi-monthly payments; their mortgage was up for renewal in about five months. They had about $2,500 in their chequing account, and had put about $20,000 aside in a rainy day fund.

But the Youngs also had an unsecured line of credit with an outstanding balance of $18,000 and credit card debt of $4,500. Their 20-year life insurance term was about to expire, and they had not made any other provisions for income replacement if anything happened to either of them. If Mel was killed in a car accident on the way to work, the insurance would pay off the mortgage but $140,000 wouldn't last long in Molly's retirement and her income wouldn't allow her to save.

Here are Mel's original projections, based on their current retirement savings:

♟

$125,000..Current RRSP (Mel's)
$10,000..RRSP contribution
$15,000..LIRA (Molly's)

$150,000..Total retirement savings

Mel believed that an average annual return projection of 8% per year was reasonable and that he and Molly could make average annual contributions of $5,400 per year up to and including the year he turned 65, for a total of about $675,000 at retirement. (Mel's contribution for the current year was higher because of the extraordinary amount of overtime he'd worked last year.)

Mel, Molly and I originally met in 2002 when the economy and stock markets were still growing. But as we know today, the stock market does not always perform as we'd like or even as we expect it to. For that reason, it's important to realize that projected returns are just that – projections. For example, if Mel had used 6% for his projections, he and Molly would theoretically have saved about $520,000 at retirement.

For the sake of consistency, however, I will use 8% as our projected average annual return, except later in the book, when I will outline worst-case scenarios. Such a return isn't far-fetched. According to a mutual fund company called Vanguard, a portfolio consisting of 50% stocks and 50% bonds averaged 8.4% annually between 1926 and 2007, with negative returns in 16 of those years.

To have the retirement they wanted, with the annual golf trip and the Caribbean cruise, Mel and Molly knew they needed to save a lot more. But they had no extra money to do so, unless they sacrificed the lifestyle they enjoyed today. And like a lot of people, they weren't willing to gamble today's pleasures. They understood that life is short and precious. Just in case one or the other of them didn't live long enough or wasn't healthy enough to enjoy retirement, they wanted to enjoy themselves today.

We've all heard about the "Latte Factor," the idea that you can find the money to save by cutting down on your daily expenses. And while that can make a difference for some people, in my experience, most people aren't willing to forgo their vacation or the Friday night beer and wings over the long term. It's like going on a diet – it's possible, and most of us can manage to lose 10 pounds when we have to. But over time, we go back to our old ways. It's human nature.

THE PAYOFF

Luckily, as I told Mel and Molly, a financial diet wasn't necessary. We were going to get human nature working for us. In fact, with the process I outlined for them, we took money that would otherwise go to the banks and the government and used it to create a much more comfortable retirement.

This is why I became a financial advisor and why I love my job so much. The Youngs needed my help, and I knew I could help them achieve the retirement of their dreams without giving up the life they enjoyed today.

With our process, Mel and Molly were about to begin:

- Paying off their mortgage faster
- Contributing more to their retirement accounts – substantially more
- Saving (a lot) on their income taxes
- Maintaining an emergency fund and appropriate insurance coverage
- Funding their own guaranteed Personal Pension Plan

And they could still enjoy their annual vacations. Like Hank and Linda, they just needed to follow the *Dessanomics* plan. ("*Dessanomics*" was coined by one of our office team members, and I thought it was perfect shorthand for our system.)

In summary, here are Mel and Molly's goals:

- To pay off their house as quickly as possible
- To have an annual retirement income of at least $75,000

Mel and Molly's situation is similar to that shared by tens of thousands of Canadian boomers, and if you were born between 1945 and 1964, you may be among them. In order to change your financial picture from one like Mel and Molly's to one more like Hank and Linda's, it's important that you begin by understanding three things:

1. How much money is going where every month
2. How much you will get back in tax refunds
3. How you can stop paying non-tax-deductible interest and start earning instead

In other words, you need to become very clear on your cash flow before and after tax. To begin, we first have to understand the nature of debt.

Mel and Molly were naturally sceptical when I promised them a way to build wealth faster by using the interest and taxes they'd save by applying *Dessanomics*. But by the end of our second meeting, as you will see later, they were convinced. And a few years later, they were delighted with the progress they were making on their net worth statement.

If you stay with me for the next nine chapters, I think you will be, too.

Chapter 2:
UNDERSTANDING DEBT

■ ■ ■

If I had to name a single factor that prevents Canadians from realizing their retirement dreams, it would be the way we use debt. Too many people just don't know the difference between good debt and bad debt, and that simple misunderstanding keeps us much poorer than we need to be.

Like you, probably, the Youngs had a mortgage. A mortgage is good debt, and I'll tell you why in a moment. But the problem is that the Youngs also had an outstanding balance on their line of credit and credit card debt – bad debt.

To make sure you don't get caught in the debt trap, remember these *Dessanomics* keys:

WHEN YOU INCUR DEBT TO GAIN WEALTH (AS WITH A MORTGAGE), THAT'S A GOOD THING.

Dessanomics
KEY:
2

WHEN YOU INCUR DEBT TO GAIN WEALTH AND GET A TAX REFUND, THAT'S A REALLY GOOD THING. BORROWING TO INVEST, COMMONLY KNOWN AS LEVERAGING, IS AN EXAMPLE.

Dessanomics
KEY:
3

WHEN YOU INCUR DEBT JUST BECAUSE YOU WANT A REALLY SPECIAL BOTTLE OF WINE FOR YOUR ANNIVERSARY DINNER, OR FOR ANY PURPOSE OTHER THAN BUILDING WEALTH, THAT'S A BAD THING.

Bad debt is very bad. It keeps way too many Canadians trapped in a downward spiral of financial anxiety and powerlessness, unable to get ahead.

To compound matters, we tend to put bad debt on our credit cards, pay minimum payments at a very high rate of interest (up to 30% on department store credit cards) and take our time paying them off.

But at the same time, Canadians hate mortgages, so even though we have an asset that is appreciating in value, and a very low rate of interest, we often make accelerated payments.

I continually see people who proudly tell me they don't have a mortgage and then tell me they do have a very large line of credit and other debt.

Does this make sense to you? Why would someone pay off her least expensive debt (good debt) and not pay off the most expensive debt (bad debt)?

Your aim should always be to accumulate the highest net worth at the lowest possible cost. With *Dessanomics*, we focus on getting rid of bad debt fast (in some cases, almost instantly), while using lower income tax and beneficial debt – at low interest rates – to build wealth.

In my experience, the reason most people fall into the trap of paying low interest debt off first is that no one has taken the time to show them how they could benefit from a change in their payment pattern. No one has ever taken the time to help them set up their debts and debt repayment plan more efficiently.

> After nearly 14 years in the banking industry, I was very familiar with all the strategies we've all been told to do to help build wealth. Although the strategies were rooted in common sense, they didn't really do much to help, and there hasn't been anything new in years. Until now. With Dessanomics, for the first time it all actually made sense to me. And, I could finally see how this was possible in my life.
>
> **THE FORMER BANK EMPLOYEE WHO'S STILL LEARNING "THE BIZ"**

We're going to change that today. Now that you understand you can have good debt, better debt, and bad debt, you're probably eager to find a plan that can help you pay off bad debt faster (using less of your money and more of the government's money) and get your balance sheet operating in a much more efficient manner.

Let's take a look at what happened with Mel and Molly. The Youngs had equity in their home. When I met with them, the fair market value was $300,000. Their mortgage was $125,000, so in lending terms, they had $175,000 in home equity. ($300,000 fair market value minus $125,000 mortgage = home equity.)

That equity was the result of their hard work and efforts to pay down their mortgage. The market value of their home had also increased since they first purchased it. While home prices are down from the highs reached in 2006 and 2007, most Canadian homeowners still have home equity.

NEVER, EVER PAY OFF THE GOOD DEBT FIRST.

According to Statistics Canada, by the end of 2005, the value of principal residences comprised 33% of the total $5.6 trillion total wealth of Canadians. By comparison, the second largest asset was employer pension plans, which represented only 18.5% of all assets.

The same study found that the Canadian debt load reached $760 billion in 2005, nearly 1.5 times more than in 1999, and only 75% of this amount was mortgage debt.

Two of the most important questions borrowers can ask themselves are, "Am I paying off my mortgage by putting living expenses on my credit cards? Am I paying off my mortgage by neglecting to save for my retirement?"

In Mel and Molly's case, their answer was yes, and yes. So I introduced them to:

ENDING THE BALANCE SHEET TWO-STEP

One thing I know from years of studying human nature is that we don't always act rationally, and the *Dessanomics* process was designed with human nature in mind. Let's go back to Chapter 1 when we met the Youngs – smart, responsible people who were paying about $2,300 a year for the illusion of saving while carrying the same amount in high interest debt. Not logical, right? But very, very common.

You will remember from Chapter 1 that the Youngs also had some cash: $20,000 in a GIC and $2,500 in their savings account, for a total of $22,500.

They were confused when I asked them, "Why in the world would you pay interest on money you don't owe?"

Okay. I've lost you now, too, I know. But let's think this through together.

The Youngs had $22,500 on deposit at the bank. On both their GIC and savings account, they were receiving a very low rate of interest, less than 3%. They owed the bank a total of $22,500, $18,000 on a line of credit (at about 7.5% interest) and $4,500 in credit card debt at about 18% interest.

In other words, the Youngs owed the bank nothing but were paying almost 10% in interest every year (over $2,100!) for the privilege.

This is the situation that tens of thousands of Canadians are in today.

On top of the interest they were needlessly paying, they were also losing the opportunity to build wealth with the money they were using to pay off debt. That added up to payments of $600 each month when I met them ($350 on the line of credit and $250 on the credit cards.)

To add insult to injury, Mel had to pay income tax on the interest he earned on the GIC and savings account – an added tax bill of about $300 each year.

If you're in a similar situation, and chances are you are, why not keep that money in your pocket? (Are you thinking about what you would do with that extra money? A trip to Cabo? A down payment on your bathroom renovation? Stop daydreaming! We still have a lot of work to do. You don't have the money yet, but stay with me, and you soon will.)

With a line of credit that amalgamates all your debt and savings, the bottom line is always the bottom line, and it is staring you right in the face. Nobel Prize-winning economist Daniel Kahneman, one of the founders of the now popular field of behavioural finance, wrote about the phenomena of "mental accounts." According to his work, "there is a behavioural phenomenon of not consolidating debt because of 'Sticker Shock.'" In other words, we don't consolidate our debt even when we know it could save us a significant amount of money on interest, because it is easier to cope mentally with smaller amounts in different accounts.

If you're feeling a little woozy thinking about the $2,400 Mel and Molly were needlessly paying every year, you will want to sit down.

Because that is nothing compared to the $27,000 in taxes Mel had needlessly paid. Yes, with $60,000 in unused contribution room, Mel paid Canada Revenue Agency $27,000 in unnecessary taxes – and lost the compound returns he would have enjoyed if he'd kept and invested the debt repayments.

Like Mel and Molly when I first outlined *Dessanomics* for them, you may be thinking that it is unrealistic to use your savings to pay off your line of credit; that you need money in savings for things like FOOD if you lose your job or something goes off the rails. You may also be thinking, like Mel and Molly, that if you had $60,000, you would definitely catch up on your RRSP contributions, but you just don't have it.

That's exactly the kind of thinking that keeps so many Canadians trapped in the same situation as Mel and Molly found themselves in: doing everything their financial advisors and bankers tell them to do, but never being able to create the results they want.

In a report released October 2005, Dr. Moshe Milevsky of York University wrote, "Debt consolidation is not practiced because the magnitude of the loss is not well understood." That has been my experience as well. When I show my clients how much they could save by managing their debt more efficiently, they're stunned. The magnitude of loss is massive.

To make the most of your money, it's important to understand how balance sheets work. It's pretty simple, and the math involved is elementary. But unless you're a business owner, you've probably never thought about the importance of your personal balance sheet.

The concept is straightforward: you have two columns, one of assets and one of liabilities. The total (assets minus liabilities) is your net worth, a number that certainly concerns your bank. If your bank thinks it's important, you should too. You want that number to grow as much as possible every year, and you want that growth to cost as little as possible. (That's what we call efficient cash flow.)

ASSETS MINUS LIABILITIES = NET WORTH (A-L=NW)

ASSETS: In this column, you should list everything you own that has financial value. Things like a leased car won't appear here, and if you decide to include things like furniture, use the resale value, not the purchase price. (That's another mistake people make that keeps them from building wealth – confusing lifestyle expenses, such as a car that depreciates in value, with assets, or real wealth.) If you have items such as jewellery or art whose resale value you don't know, don't worry about it for now. Keep it simple.

Minus

LIABILITIES: Now you need to add up all of the money you owe to anyone you need to pay off at some point in the future. If you have an interest-free loan from dad, for example, and you plan to pay it back, you need to add it to the list. Include all credit card and loan balances and anything you might owe Canada Revenue Agency.

Equals

YOUR NET WORTH

Let's look at the Young's balance sheet. Feel free to pencil in your own numbers in the chart provided in order to do a quick calculation.

ASSETS — LIABILITIES

SHORT TERM

$2,500 Cash - bank account	$18,000 Line of credit
$20,000 30 day GIC	$4,500 Credit card

LONG TERM

$300,000 House market value	$125,000 Mortgage
$125,000 RRSP - Mel	
$15,000 LIRA - Molly	
$10,000 This year's RRSP	
$472,500 TOTAL ASSETS —	$147,500 TOTAL LIABILITIES

$325,000 TOTAL NET WORTH

YOUR LIST

ASSETS — LIABILITIES

SHORT TERM

_____	Cash	_____	Line of credit 1
_____	Other short term investments	_____	Line of credit 2

LONG TERM

_____	Real estate	_____	Credit card 1
_____	RRSP (yours)	_____	Credit card 2
_____	RRSP (your spouse)	_____	Credit card 3
_____	LIRA (yours)	_____	Credit card 4
_____	LIRA (your spouse)	_____	Mortgage
_____	Other investments	_____	Other ?
_____	TOTAL ASSETS —	_____	TOTAL LIABILITIES

_____ TOTAL NET WORTH

The Youngs had their debt in different accounts. They owed X on their mortgage, Y on their various credit cards and Z on their personal line of credit and car loans. Keeping everything in separate mental accounts may have been more emotionally comfortable, but it is comfort that no one can afford.

That looks pretty good, right?

But let's narrow this down a bit to get to the heart of the problem. Let's look just at the Young's short-term assets and liabilities.

SHORT TERM ASSETS	—	SHORT TERM LIABILITIES
$2,500 Cash - bank account		$18,000 Line of credit
$20,000 30 day GIC		$4,500 Credit card
$22,500 TOTAL ASSETS —		$22,500 TOTAL LIABILITIES

0.00 TOTAL NET WORTH

In other words, the Youngs were operating under the illusion that they had $22,500 in savings ($2,500 in the bank and $20,000 in short-term savings). Are you operating under a similar illusion?

The truth of the matter is the Youngs had nothing, because they owed the bank exactly that amount on their line of credit and credit card, and they were paying about $2,400 each year for that illusion.

If you think it through, it's mind-boggling to realize that the bank is charging you interest AND making you make payments to them monthly on money that you don't even owe. In addition to the unnecessary interest, Mel and Molly were paying approximately $5,100 per year ($425 per month) toward that debt, money they could have used for other things, all much more profitable or enjoyable.

Have you ever noticed that mortgage and credit card balances are always quoted in positive numbers? Now, according to accounting principles, they should appear in red, or with a negative sign beside them, or in brackets. But that would be uncomfortable! With your new "all-in-one account," you'll see the true balance of your account every time you go to the ATM. If your balance is -$249,800, and you withdraw $200 to go out for dinner, your account balance will drop to -$250,000. You'll see that your debt has just increased by $200, and that is a powerful motivator.

However, it works the same on the other side of the equation. When you deposit your $5,000 pay cheque, you immediately see a dramatic impact on your balance: -$250,000 + $5,000 = -$245,000. That is also a uniquely powerful motivator, providing a great feeling of real accomplishment.

Like many of the people I've run into over the years, Mel and Molly allowed this to happen because it gave them a false sense of security. It made them feel as if they had money they didn't have. The cost came in the form of interest and lost opportunity for money they didn't really owe!

So let's take a look again at their complete balance sheet, and see what it should have looked like:

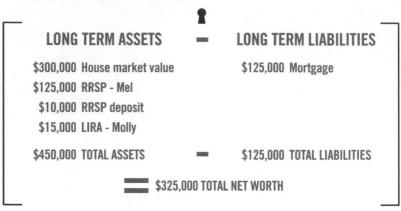

LONG TERM ASSETS	—	LONG TERM LIABILITIES
$300,000 House market value		$125,000 Mortgage
$125,000 RRSP - Mel		
$10,000 RRSP deposit		
$15,000 LIRA - Molly		
$450,000 TOTAL ASSETS	—	$125,000 TOTAL LIABILITIES
	$325,000 TOTAL NET WORTH	

As you can see, that all-important number, net worth, remained exactly the same. But what's different is what happened in the following year. The Youngs had an additional $2,400 in cash with which to build their wealth. The $600 per month payments they'd been making on the line of credit and credit card balance they now applied to wealth building.

The Youngs were paying more than $2,100 in unnecessary interest to their bank. But because banks are in the business of lending money and charging interest, you're never going to hear this from a bank.

Banks make money off the interest that you pay, and then they turn around and lend your savings to another poor, unsuspecting soul. That's what banks do. It's their job to create profits by lending money and charging interest on it, and it's your job to make sure you don't pay more than you have to. And I'm here to help you with that!

CLEAN UP YOUR BALANCE SHEET TO PAY AS LITTLE AS POSSIBLE IN INTEREST AND TAXES: DEBT IN ONE ACCOUNT AND SAVINGS IN THE OTHER EQUAL HIGHER INTEREST TO YOUR BANKER, HIGHER TAXES FOR YOUR GOVERNMENT, AND LESS WEALTH FOR YOU!

Next, let's consider how the Youngs were paying their mortgage.

Remember they were making accelerated payments. The outstanding balance was $125,000, and they were paying more than they had to, increasing their payments to $1,100 each month. This made sense to them, since they wanted to be sure the house was paid off in about 15 years, when they retired.

Earlier in the chapter, I mentioned that incurring debt to gain wealth and get a tax deduction was the best kind of debt.

What do you think might have happened if the Youngs had used all or part of the $600 they were formerly paying on their line of credit and credit card debt – and changed the way they were paying their mortgage – to acquire more wealth, reduce their income tax, and pay less tax in the future?

Wouldn't that make sense? Like the Youngs, you're learning.

WHEN YOU PAY LESS TO THE BANKS AND GOVERNMENT, YOU FREE UP CASH FLOW. WHEN YOU FREE UP CASH FLOW, YOU INCREASE YOUR ABILITY TO BUILD WEALTH.

Now that you're starting to understand net worth, let's see why cash flow is so important.

Chapter 3:

GOING WITH THE (CASH) FLOW

■ ■ ■

Before we look at the broader topic of cash flow, let's consider the garden variety mortgage.

According to a study by RBC Economics at the end of 2008, the annual costs of owning a standard two-storey house demanded about 52% of the average Canadian family income (pre-tax), while the cost of owning a condo required about 31.4% of pre-tax household income.

Our homes are usually our biggest lifetime purchase and our single biggest expense other than taxes.

Mel and Molly had locked in their mortgage for five years at what they thought was a good rate. When I first explained to them they could do a lot better, they looked at me with disbelief.

I explained that, when you invest your money, you want it compounded as often as possible, and Molly jumped in, "I remember taking that in school. Our teacher called compounding the eighth wonder of the world!"

"Yes, when you're investing, compounding is the secret to growing wealth. But when you borrow money, you don't want it compounding at all, unless you also want to pay the lender all that extra money," I said.

Mortgage interest is compounded. While the bank makes more in interest payments, you not only pay more for your mortgage, but it also takes longer to pay off the debt. As we discussed in the last chapter, that represents a lot of lost opportunity.

GOODBYE HIGH INTEREST – HELLO ALL-IN-ONE HELOC!

For some people, a mortgage is the only option. But for other people like Mel and Molly, and hopefully you, a sound credit history, home equity, job security and net worth combine to give good credit worthiness and better options. (It's one of the ironies of life – the less you need to borrow money, the more lenders want to give it to you.)

If you meet these criteria, you should consider a line of credit tied to the equity in your home as opposed to a mortgage. This will keep your interest costs down and give you much greater flexibility with your cash flow.

A home equity-backed line of credit (commonly referred to as a HELOC) is better than a mortgage for several reasons. "You may not have heard of these before," I said to Mel and Molly. Popular in Australia, they have only recently been introduced in Canada," I explained, "and are not usually available from your traditional bank."

It took a bit of convincing with Mel and Molly, because they'd just never thought about anything but the standard mortgage options.

Like most mortgage lenders, the Young's bank allowed them to pre-pay up to 15% per year. If they inherited some money, the interest on their mortgage would keep growing, even as the money sat in the bank earning very little. Conversely, even though they'd paid off a huge chunk of their mortgage, if there was a financial emergency, their bank wouldn't just let them borrow that money back again. They would have to refinance, with all the fees and hassle that goes along with that.

If the Youngs needed money for renovations or a new car, they would have to approach a lender for a loan. Even if they got the loan at the same bank, the interest rate would still be substantially higher than that on their mortgage.

So I continued my argument. "When your personal line of credit is not quite enough at the moment, you 'borrow' on your credit cards, which is even more expensive.

With a HELOC, the money you need will be available to you when you need it, at the same low rate of interest, and you will never have to pay interest on money you don't owe. You will be saving money every single day," I explained.

Are you worried that having access to a line of credit will tempt you to spend more and take on more debt? My experience shows this is not the case. But another thing you probably want to consider is this: you won't be approved for a HELOC unless you have 20% equity in your home, and a solid credit history. If you've managed your debt well to this point, what are the chances you'll suddenly develop a different, less responsible personality? *Dessanomics* is designed for people who are responsible with debt, but need a faster, more efficient way to pay it off. When the concept of "diversification of debt" and its damaging effects are widely understood, believe me, we're going to look back at the traditional methods and wonder what we were thinking.

When it comes to mortgages, many people choose a fixed rate because it feels more secure. But research conducted by Professor Moshe Milevsky at York University has proven that Canadians do better with variable rates. Analyzing data from 1950 to 2007, Dr. Milevsky found that the average Canadian could expect to save interest more than 90% of the time by choosing a variable-rate mortgage instead of a fixed. The average savings with a variable rate option was $20,630 over 15 years, per $100,000 borrowed.

This is because, over time, the average variable interest rate will be lower.

I encouraged the Youngs to pay off their mortgage when it matured, and replace it with a HELOC, giving them a lower total borrowing cost AND the flexibility to pay it off whenever they want or borrow it back whenever they need money.

By saving money in interest, we're going to free up a lot of cash – perhaps as much as hundreds of thousands of dollars – which you can then apply to something else, like investing for YOUR retirement, for example.

Add to that the fees and interest you will save by having access to low-interest credit when you need it, and you will have a very tidy sum to add to your retirement savings.

> I have worked on countless cases like the Youngs - normal, average Canadians. The average difference in their net worth over 15 to 20 years on the *Dessanomics* process is in the range of **$1,000,000** using the same income, and maintaining the same lifestyle. That is the magnitude of loss we're talking about. It's the difference between a comfortable retirement and one spent worrying about whether there will be enough to visit the kids or buy that hearing aid when it can't be put off any longer.

Another argument that eventually convinced the Youngs to make the change is the control that a HELOC gave them over their money. With a mortgage, your lender is in control. They tell you how much to pay and when, and every five years or so, you have to go back to them with your hat in hand and pay fees to arrange a new mortgage.

And because of the way mortgages are repaid, once you've made a payment, that money is no longer available to you, meaning you have to borrow at higher interest rates if you need credit. That leaves many people trapped in a cycle of paying off a car loan over four or five years, making minimum payments on credit cards, and paying off a personal line of credit over five years. With a HELOC, they can escape from this trap.

THE DOWNSIDE OF DIVERSIFICATION

Most Canadians understand that diversification is important when it comes to their investments. But diversification is a killer when it comes to debt and savings.

Consolidation is the better alternative. And that's what you get with a HELOC. These are usually offered at very low rates. (In mid-December 2008, the rate was 3.5%.)

A HELOC is secured by the equity in your home, and you can use up to your maximum borrowing limit, which is determined by your home's value and your home equity.

In the Youngs' case, they had plenty of equity in their home ($300,000 market value minus $125,000 mortgage = $175,000 home equity).

I showed them that, if we secured a HELOC, it would be at an 80% "loan to value" ratio. In other words, they could secure a line of credit, at a low rate, for 80% of the value of their home ($300,000). So in addition to paying off their $125,000 mortgage, they would have access to another $115,000 in case of financial emergencies. (That is one huge emergency fund!)

"I don't know how we feel about another $115,000 of debt," said Mel.

"It isn't debt unless you spend the money," I replied. "Remember your balance sheet."

"Yes, but we could spend it," said Mel.

I agreed. I run into this concern each and every time I recommended a HELOC.

While it is true that someone could theoretically use their income tax refund to buy a sailboat rather than pay down her HELOC, once people have seen this plan in action, it's hard to resist. And in case someone did decide to extend the life of their debt by spending her tax and interest savings elsewhere, she'd still be in a better position by virtue of her balance sheet.

To reassure them, I asked Mel and Molly to list the credit cards they had and the maximum limit on each one. This was their list, which in my experience, resembles most families' credit card lists.

- Molly's Sears $10,000
- Molly's Visa $20,000
- Joint Mastercard $15,000
- Mel's Visa $20,000
- Mel's Canadian Tire $5,000

I already knew the maximum on the Young's personal line of credit was $50,000, so their total available credit was $120,000. In other words, they already had more credit available than they would on their HELOC, and if they were really concerned, they had the option of closing those credit accounts after the HELOC was arranged.

But I didn't share their concern, because after working for many years with many hundreds of people, I knew people like Mel and Molly don't manage to get where they are in life without knowing how to manage their household expenses and credit. There are people who shouldn't have access to credit, but if you've managed to develop home equity and assets, it's very unlikely you're among them.

> " We can't thank you enough for the opportunity to participate in your Wealth Building Strategy. The financial plan and strategies you have designed are incredible, allowing us to pay off our mortgage in a fraction of the time, while securing our future so we can enjoy our retirement to its fullest. Without your guidance we would never have realized the savings potential. "
>
> THE BEAUTY SUPPLY SALES MANAGER & THE FOOD INDUSTRY KEENER

"The only difference," I told Mel and Molly, "is that, with a HELOC, the credit will be available – if you need it – at a much lower rate of interest."

"Dessa, are you saying we should close down our line of credit and some or all of our credit cards and roll them into a low-interest line of credit? Would that give us the flexibility and lower interest rate you were talking about?" asked Mel.

"Yes. And you will need to roll in your mortgage as well," I replied.

"But we're already paying that off at an accelerated rate," said Mel.

"Yes, but remember you'll probably end up paying fees when your mortgage comes up for renewal. You don't want that. And, I want you to free up even more cash flow."

Mel and Molly nodded in unison. I could see we were making progress.

Dessanomics

KEY: 7

DIVERSIFIED INVESTMENTS ARE GREAT. DIVERSIFIED DEBTS ARE EXPENSIVE AND INEFFICIENT. AN ALL-IN-ONE HOME EQUITY LINE OF CREDIT (HELOC) ALLOWS YOU TO PAY LESS INTEREST AND PAY DEBTS FASTER.

THINKING LIKE A BUSINESS

"Most Canadian families would do a lot better if they managed their personal finances the same way a small business does. A small business secures a line of credit at the bank, and only draws on it when necessary. The bank charges them interest only on the portion they use, for the time they use it. Now doesn't that make more sense?" I asked.

"But we're not a business," said Molly.

"That's true, but there are many similarities," I said. "You earn money by selling your services to your employer, then you deposit that money into a bank account and pay all of your operating expenses. When you have money left over at the end of the year, you are..."

"Profitable!" said Molly.

"Exactly. So if you were a business, what would you look for?" I asked.

"Well, businesses seem to have a lot more tax write-offs than we do," said Molly. "I don't think they use credit cards for their operating expenses, and I think they get better interest rates when they borrow."

"You bet," I said.

Mel and Molly were catching on, and I could see them both getting more enthusiastic as they started to see the benefits.

"I know that when they deposit money to their bank accounts," Molly said, "the first thing the bank does is pay down the operating line, if they are overdrawn. When I was an accounts payable clerk, my boss always told me to keep a careful eye on our operating line."

"And why was that?" I asked, smiling.

"Because he saved money that way," said Molly.

BINGO!

> This powerful, immediate reinforcement is usually enough not only to keep my clients on track with their plan, but also to do more, faster, and spend less in order to enjoy the real satisfaction of immediate wealth creation.

"So," I said, "we should set up a line of credit, use it only when necessary, and have total control over when and how we make principal payments."

The Young's mortgage was up for renewal in a few months, so they didn't have to pay a penalty to get out. However, even if they had to pay a penalty to improve their debt management, I would have recommended it.

Remember the cost of borrowing?

The interest rate on the Young's mortgage was 6.5% with an outstanding balance of approximately $125,000. The normal penalty to pay this out is usually three times the monthly interest. For the Youngs, that would have been about $2,000. Ouch! But wait a minute. By lowering the interest rate from 6.5% to 3.5%, they would have saved over $900 in the first three months, and $3,750 in the first year.

Actually, the savings would have been even higher, but that is complicated math, the kind we're trying to avoid.

> Until now, there simply was no way to stop the financial hemorrhage, but between the new products that have been recently introduced such as all-in-one HELOCs, Guaranteed Minimum Withdrawal Benefits (GMWBs), which I'll talk about later, and this process, it's time for a new era of wealth creation.

A word of warning: Be sure to check with your lender to see what the actual penalty will be when you pay off your mortgage. Some lenders charge the higher of three months interest or the difference between the current average interest rate for your term and the interest rate you agreed to pay them. And for future reference, never agree to a mortgage that includes this extortionate penalty in the fine print!

Even when your current mortgage rate is equal to or lower than the prime rate, the savings in interest can be substantial when you include all of your savings and borrowing in the same account. **A Manulife report found that you would need a mortgage at about prime minus 2% to achieve the same savings.** In today's market, that would be a 1.5% mortgage. Has your bank ever offered you a 1.5% mortgage? What do you think the chances are that it will?

Obviously, accounts that allow you to combine all of your borrowing and savings aren't available everywhere. You have to have a solid credit rating as well as 20% equity in your home.

But once you open this type of account, you can combine all of your savings and borrowing. When your pay cheque is deposited, it reduces the loan balance and your borrowing cost. When you buy your groceries, your borrowing cost increases. It's the teeter-totter approach: the account value goes up, and the account value goes down. Over time, it makes a significant difference. And you get to spend the money you save on interest and taxes on other things, like investments, paying off your mortgage and Hank's Harley Davidson.

"So how do we do this?" asked Mel.

> In every area of our life, real positive change happens when we get real with ourselves. And there is no better way to get real with our finances than an all-in-one account.

I laid out the steps for them, one at a time:

1. Secure a large line of credit on your home, 80% loan-to-value (as noted earlier, that's 80% of your home's current market value).

2. Buy out your existing mortgage, penalty and all if necessary.

3. Roll in all your other debt such as your line of credit, credit cards, and car loan (unless it happens to be a 0% financing deal).

4. Deposit all of your savings. "Remember, as we discussed, until you have paid off all debt, your savings are an illusion," I said to Mel. "You owe as much as you have in savings, so to reduce your interest cost as much as possible, deposit all your savings into this new, all-in-one account."

5. Pay interest only to free up cash flow.

Like Mel and Molly, you probably choked, literally or figuratively, when you came to number 5.

Does this process work for everyone? So far, in my experience, yes it does, with one exception. I had a client family in which one spouse was very controlling and could never get past the idea that his spouse could withdraw funds from their account without his permission. They'd argue about whether she'd paid too much for toilet paper. Eventually, they resolved their problems by divorcing. By that point, even I agreed it was the best solution to their problems. But the good news was that they'd been practicing *Dessanomics* for several years before they separated – so they had substantially more assets to divide!

Pay interest only to free up cash flow?! Don't pay off debt as fast as possible? Pay interest for longer than you have to?

As I asked of the Youngs, please be patient. Remember Hank and Linda, and how well they were doing? That's what we're working to achieve for the Youngs, and perhaps for you.

For now, I can tell you we are going to pay off your home equity line of credit faster than you can imagine using, in part, the taxes you are going to save by applying the rest of the *Dessanomics* principles. Are you still with me?

I'll explain more about how we do it in the next chapters. This is why you do it:

- Because YOU free up cash flow
- Because YOU will have the cheapest home financing possible, period
- Because YOU are in control
- Because YOU, not your bank decide when to pay your HELOC off
- Because YOU decide how much of the principal you're going to pay off at any given time, without penalty
- Because YOU increase your borrowing only when you need the money
- Because YOU receive the highest interest equivalent on your savings
- Because YOU can take it with you when you move

MOST IMPORTANTLY

- Because YOU will have the engine to make YOU wealthy
- Because YOU can make that engine run as hard as YOU want

You may be thinking that, while this sounds good for Mel and Molly, you've paid off your mortgage, and so it doesn't apply. If so, congratulations!

But think about this thoroughly before you move on. A home equity line of credit may be just the right vehicle for building wealth for you, too.

What if:

- YOU need to borrow money in case of emergency
- YOU want to protect yourself from title fraud
- YOU want to receive the highest interest rate on your savings
- YOU want liquidity for your short-term cash savings
- YOU want access to your high interest savings account from anywhere in the world
- YOU want to use some of the equity in your home to pay for medical expenses
- YOU want to use your home equity to lend some money to your kids
- YOU want to use this for income instead of a reverse mortgage because it's cheaper and more flexible.
- YOU want to…

I could go on forever, but it's time to get back to why effective cash flow management is such an important element of wealth creation.

"
The account that *Dessanomics* recommended for us is like the ultimate all-inclusive vacation from financial stress! All of our finances are handled through that account — our savings, our mortgage, our bills — it's just so easy. The best part is watching how quickly our debt is being reduced. It's going to save us thousands!
"

THE COMPUTER GEEK MANAGER
& THE CHIROPRACTOR

Chapter 4:

EFFICIENT CASH IS KING

■ ■ ■

The Young's previous financial advisor had created a financial plan for them based on their retirement dreams. To have enough to live those dreams in retirement, the advisor told them they had to save an additional $5,000 per month.

The Youngs thought that was ridiculous, and so do I. The fact of the matter is that a financial plan provides answers based on the information you feed it in the first place. What their previous advisor recommended may have been the only option then, but new products in the marketplace have changed things.

It was obvious the Youngs were not capable of finding any more money in their current budget to save for retirement. Mel made it perfectly clear he was not going to give up his golf trip with the boys, and Molly wanted to continue her annual cruise with Mel.

By the time I met them, you may recall, their dreams for retirement were simply to have $75,000 in income each year and to have their mortgage paid off.

Based on where they were when they came to see me, there was no way they could achieve this goal.

Their strategy, you might remember, was to accelerate payments on the mortgage so it would be paid off in approximately 15 years. Their investment strategy was to add another $5,400 each year to their RRSPs.

Adding to their RRSPs every year was important to their wealth accumulation, but to achieve the income they wanted, they needed to do more, and they needed to do it more often.

Although they understood how paying their mortgage twice a month helped them pay it off a lot faster, they neglected to apply the same strategy to their RRSP. Mel contributed $150 each month, but for some reason, he'd set up his savings so that the balance, about $300 each month, was accumulated in a savings plan and set aside for contribution at the end of the year.

I suggested that Mel and Molly change things a bit. When you see the effect, I think you will want to apply these ideas, too. So let's begin by taking a closer look at the Young's major monthly payments.

$1,100	Mortgage
$350	Personal line of credit
$250	Credit card
$600	Savings ($300 savings, $300 RSP at end of year)
$150	RRSP
$2,450	Sub total
(-$205)	Tax refund for total RRSP contribution (including annual contribution)
= $2,245	Net payments

To make a true comparison, you will note I've added back the tax refund that Mel received for his total annual RRSP contribution.

Things were about to change for Mel and Molly. We were about to consolidate all of their debt to a home equity line of credit (HELOC), on which they'd be required to pay interest only. (Remember, we had a plan in mind for paying off the principle, too, but we'll get to that later.)

So, their monthly debt payments were going to be substantially reduced. In fact, for their mortgage of $125,000, the monthly payment would drop from $1,100 to only $470 if the rate averaged 4.5%. That's a difference of $630 per month.

For those of you who are still worried about variable interest rates, you may find it comforting to hear that interest rates would have to increase to 16% before the Young's monthly payment requirements would exceed those of their traditional mortgage. And that's before we even get to the benefits of tax efficiency!

When I first outlined this for Mel and Molly, he immediately balked. "Well, that's great," he said, "but I'm not paying down my mortgage. Isn't that the whole point?"

I explained I wasn't quite done. "Let's talk about your savings strategy," I said. "You contribute $150 every month to your RRSP, and $600 goes to your high-interest savings account, the one you pay tax on. At the end of the year, you top up your RRSP, and continue to grow your emergency fund. Agreed?"

"Yes," said Mel. "You're suggesting I do it differently?"

"Let's try contributing directly to your RRSP, Mel, and see what happens," I replied.

$470	HELOC[1] (Interest-only $125,000)
$1,200	RRSP
$1,670	Sub total
(-$550)	Less the RRSP refund ($1,200 x 46%)
= $1,120	Net payments

[1] We've calculated interest at 4.5%. At the time of writing, the interest rate was 3.5%, but this calculation reflects potential increases over time.

"Wow," said Molly. "We will be saving over $1,100 each month, yet we're putting more in the RRSP, and getting more tax back. I suppose we're going to pay down the line of credit with the savings?"

I could see from the look on her face that she was doing the calculations in her head.

"Holy smokes! Eleven hundred dollars a month means we'll pay off more than $13,000 of the principal balance each year," she said. "We could have it paid in less than 10 years!"

"Yes," I said, smiling.

I wanted to let that sink in a little bit. Mel and Molly were starting to understand how important efficient cash flow is in reducing costs and adding to long-term wealth.

"It's all about paying yourself first," I said. "Most people have heard that, but they don't know how to do it effectively. And we still have work to do. Remember, you could increase your tax refunds if you caught up on your RRSP contribution room, and your life insurance is going to expire. And we haven't even talked about critical illness insurance coverage yet."

Mel was looking a bit dreamy, but that reality check brought him back to the conversation.

"This is why Hank and Linda are never worried about making their RRSP contribution in the last week of February, isn't it? I think I'm starting to understand. The **TYPE** of debt we have, **HOW** we pay for it, and the **ORDER** in which we do things can have a huge impact. That's what you mean by efficient cash flow."

"That's exactly what I mean," I said. "But it gets even better. Remember when we talked about the magic of compounding? The sooner you get your money invested, the more you will make, especially if those earnings are sheltered from tax. For example, if you contribute $1,000 to your RRSP each month, as opposed to $12,000 at the end of each year over the next 15 years – assuming an 8% rate of return – you'd have almost $22,500 more without adding a single extra dollar.

"But that isn't the only benefit," I continued. "If you contribute at the beginning of each month, your money will be working for you for an extra 30 days each month, and you will benefit from dollar cost averaging as well."

They both looked a little confused, so I explained that dollar cost averaging allows investors to average out the price of the units purchased over time. You pay the same amount each month, but when the price of a unit drops because of the normal fluctuations of the market, you can buy more units.

We'd made a lot of progress. By making these simple changes – with no sacrifice in lifestyle or security – the Youngs were much closer to their retirement dreams. If we assumed an 8% return, they'd have approximately $800,000 in their RRSPs by the time Mel reached 65. (And of course, they'd be mortgage-free even earlier than that!)

"Okay," said Mel. "I think I'm clear. When can we get started?"

"Soon," I replied. "But your plan wouldn't be complete without talking about hedging your risks, and I'll also suggest some tax strategies I think you're really going to like."

"You mean there's more?" said Mel. "No wonder Hank and Linda are so far ahead of us."

But what I didn't say to the Youngs at that point is that our plan still wouldn't create the $75,000 of after-tax income they wanted each year in retirement. If their retirement fund earned average annual returns of 5%, they'd run out of money in year 19, even if they withdrew just $65,000 in before-tax income.

> Many advisors do retirement planning projections based on a theoretical date of death. If it was possible to predict date of death, this job would be a whole lot easier.
>
> But that is what I was taught to do when I trained as a financial advisor.

After working with many, many clients over the years, I'm convinced that most people, like me, would prefer not to worry about their money running out before they do. No one wants to contemplate bouncing cheques at 91 because his retirement plan ran out at 90. Most people would prefer to leave a little something to their children, or to their favourite charities.

That's what I was about to suggest for Mel and Molly. As you will see in the next chapters, it is possible – for them, and for you.

Dessanomics

KEY: 8

MANY PEOPLE TRY TO "PAY THEMSELVES FIRST" WHEN THEY'RE SAVING FOR RETIREMENT, BUT REALLY, THEY'RE STANDING THIRD IN LINE BEHIND THEIR LENDERS AND THE TAXMAN. *DESSANOMICS* IS THE ONLY SYSTEM THAT PUTS YOU AT THE FRONT OF THE LINE!

Chapter 5:

ENSURING YOUR SINGLE GREATEST ASSET – YOUR EARNING POWER

■ ■ ■

I nsurance for Mel and Molly is their hedge against the possibility that Mel can't earn any more income.

If you remember from Chapter 1, Mel and Molly each had $150,000 of 20-year term life insurance, about to expire in a few months. The current premium was $45 a month, but they could renew for another term or convert all or part of it to a permanent type. It also contained a guaranteed new premium of $115 a month. We needed to make some decisions.

Before we talked about that, though, Mel dropped a dusty, leather-bound folio into my lap. "Here – is this worth anything? My great aunt Patsy gave it to me years ago, and I've kept it in the safety deposit box ever since."

Opening up the folio, I suspected what it could be, and sure enough, it was a baby policy, life insurance on Mel that was purchased when he was a baby. As advisors we see these types of policies from time to time, usually purchased by a grandparent or some other member of the family with the intent to save some money for the benefit of the child at some point in the future. Mel's Great Aunt Patsy had died several years earlier. Her estate was left to her children, but she did Mel a favour.

"Do you know what this is, Mel?" I asked. Nodding his head, he mumbled, "Yes, but it can't be worth much of anything. Patsy did that almost 50 years ago."

Molly said, "You were always her favourite. I bet it's worth something. She was shrewd with her money. Look at how well she did after your Uncle Pete died."

"Mel, this is a paid-up policy, worth a little over $100,000!" I exclaimed.

"God bless Aunt Patsy!" Mel said, smiling broadly. "I guess I really was her favourite. This is my lucky day. Wait till I tell Hank. I guess we won't have to worry too much about that other insurance now, will we?"

Did the Youngs need to continue with their insurance, or could we drop it and save the $45 a month (increasing to $115 a month) premium?

You may say drop it, because we have been trying to free up cash flow. In this case, however, the premium is money well spent, and it should not be used for anything else. Mel and Molly still owed money on their debt obligations, and they didn't yet have enough in investments to sustain the family for long.

Mel did have some group coverage from his work – $180,000 – plus he had a little bit of group from the fire department – another $25,000, which, combined with the $100,000 from Aunt Patsy and his personal term policy (the one about to expire), amounted to a total of $455,000.

> I believe that the biggest reason most Canadians are not looking to insurance as part of their personal financial package is because they believe they can't afford yet another expense. If you can't find the money to pay for it, it doesn't matter how important it may be.

Usually I do not like to use group insurance in my analysis, because it can be cancelled at the discretion of the employer or lost when employment ends.

But in Mel's case, I didn't mind including it. He had been in the same job for almost 20 years, and the company was secure. It was very unlikely he'd lose his job in the next few years, even though his overtime might change with the economy.

As well, I thought it was important to use every extra dollar for wealth creation. In other words, to have enough insurance, but no more.

There are many ways to assess how much life insurance a person needs. I'm going to give you a very simple version, using some very simple math.

Here are Mel and Molly's expenses and debts:

$125,000   Mortgage on the house
$18,000   Line of credit
$4,500   Credit card debt
$15,000   Final expenses
$50,000   RRSP top up
(-$27,600)   Less RRSP refund

$184,900   Total

This is the insurance that Mel had:

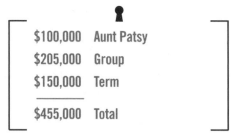

$100,000   Aunt Patsy
$205,000   Group
$150,000   Term

$455,000   Total

The way many people would interpret this is that Mel had $455,000 in insurance benefits, minus the $184,900 required to pay off all the debt, which would leave Molly $270,100 to invest and live on. The math is right, but there is a glaring flaw in the reasoning.

Think of it this way. We know that Molly made about $30,000 per year. With the CPP spousal benefit of $4,300 per year, she would have had $34,300 per year of income after Mel's death. My analysis showed that she would need an income of $70,000 per year (after tax) to pay living expenses and stay in her home.

If Molly were short $35,700 each year, how long do you think $270,000 of insurance money would have lasted? Depending on the rate of return she'd get on the money, it would last seven or eight years, or even 10. Here's the problem and here's where an advisor can really help.

In Mel and Molly's case, we needed to accomplish at least three objectives:

1. Pay off debt.
2. Set aside a capital pool so that Molly could draw down income until she was ready to retire.
3. Set aside another capital pool to provide income when Molly retired.

Molly needed money to provide income now and in the future.

Our insurance-needs analysis showed that Mel needed another $250,000 of insurance on top of the current amount of $455,000 that he had.

Molly, on the other hand, needed about $165,000, and they were very close on that number with their existing term policy.

We considered how much it would cost if we renewed their current coverage for another 20 years through their existing policy, knowing we could cancel it in 15 years when the debt was paid and assets were built up, and then added a new policy for the other $250,000 that Mel needed. Or we could look at the cost of a whole new policy.

A word to the wise: when you're buying insurance, the more people you include in a plan, the better. There is a fee for each policy, so if you purchase separate policies for each of your family members, they will each incur a fee. You can save money by putting everyone on the same policy.

The other option for Mel and Molly was to rewrite their insurance, which would require them both to go through medicals. If this worked, we could save them money, because term rates have fallen in recent years. It was much cheaper than it was 20 years ago to get the same coverage.

If Mel and Molly proved to be healthy, they would be able to get a bigger bang for their buck – more coverage for less money.

I believe strongly that, while we are acquiring assets and paying off non-deductible debt, we need the least expensive type of insurance. There may be a need later for some type of permanent insurance for estate protection or tax management, but that wasn't the case for Mel and Molly.

The common financial planning adage, "buy term and invest the difference," definitely applied to them. Term insurance is the most cash-flow efficient. It is there to meet a specific, important need: in this case, protecting Mel's family from the loss of his income-earning power in the event of his death. In addition, their term insurance would be convertible at a later date to a permanent type without any medicals, if they needed the coverage.

There are very beneficial uses for permanent insurance (such as the policy Aunt Patsy purchased for Mel), but that is a subject for another book. Mel and Molly might need it for estate planning and to shelter as much of their retirement portfolio from tax as possible.

In the meantime, Mel and Molly agreed to submit to new medical exams, which in this case, were nothing more than basic tests. If my plan worked, and they proved to be healthy, they could acquire a new policy for only $85 per month – $30 per month less than their current policy, which did not in any case provide enough coverage for their needs.

"More coverage, less money. Now that's something I really like," muttered Mel. "I like the idea that, if something happens to me, Molly's retirement plans will still be on track. But that only works if I die, right? What happens if I have a heart attack, or a stroke? Or if I get cancer? Or if Molly gets cancer? It runs in her family."

QUALITY OF LIFE INSURANCE

There is an old joke in the industry that life insurance should more accurately be called death insurance, but it just wouldn't sell.

The fact is, people don't buy life insurance for themselves. They buy it out of love, so that the people who depend on them won't be left in poverty as well as grief.

But with longer life expectancies, it is now far more likely we will suffer from a critical illness than die prematurely. For example, according to the Canadian Cancer Society, 39% of Canadian women and 45% of Canadian men will suffer from cancer during their lifetimes. According to the National Cancer Institute of Canada, 60% of those people will survive – up from only 25% in the 1940s. And according the Canadian Heart & Stroke Foundation, one in four Canadians will experience heart disease; 50% of people who have heart attacks are under 65. Fifty thousand Canadians have a stroke each year, and 75% survive the initial event.

While increasing survival rates are good news, the financial reality of those statistics can be devastating.

That was really brought home for me when the wife of a friend I play golf with was diagnosed with breast cancer last year. Like many people who get cancer, Kathleen didn't see it coming. She was healthy, fit and barely into middle age.

While she and her family were dealing with the devastating emotional impact of learning she had cancer and the side effects of the treatments she was receiving, they got one more blow. The medication her doctors recommended as her best bet for beating the disease after surgery wasn't covered by the government health plan.

The cost? Three thousand dollars a month for a year or more.

When I played golf recently with Kathleen's husband, Bob, he told me they're still uncertain when she'll be able to get back to work. As is the case for a lot of people who receive cancer treatment, the after-effects have left Kathleen unable to do her job, at least for the immediate future. And the company she works for just changed its policy about keeping positions open for employees who are ill. If she isn't back to work within a year, she may lose her job.

It's bad enough that you get cancer. It's terrible that you might have to use your retirement savings to pay for the treatment. But to have to think about getting your resumé in order to look for a new job when you finally recover? It's ludicrous.

When I work with clients like Mel and Molly these days, I think about Kathleen and Bob. As I said to Mel, your group disability policy covers only your income, but if you have a critical illness, you may also have a whole new set of expenses. As well, the fine print in your disability policy may mean you have to return to work when you can – as opposed to when you're ready – or lose your income.

> Critical illness insurance is something I want all of my clients to consider while we are in the wealth creation mode. With our ever-changing medical system, I believe it is essential to include this in any financial plan.

"The risk of getting a critical illness is so high, Mel, that I believe you need something more than life insurance, which helps only when you're dead, and disability insurance, which only replaces your income. You're likely to have a whole new set of expenses."

> You shouldn't have to be struggling to manage your finances when you're fighting for your life! Peace of mind – it's a precious thing.
>
> **THE ENGINEER & BREAST CANCER SURVIVOR**

"I agree," said Molly. "I've always thought that if one of us found out we had cancer, I'd want to spend time recovering someplace where we could really relax. It seems to me that's an important part of getting well – being able to get away from worries and responsibilities and really rest."

"That's one of the great things about critical illness insurance," I said. "It pays a lump sum – tax-free – that can be used for anything you want to use it for. If your doctor recommends treatment that isn't covered by your provincial health care plan, or if you want to spend some time in Florida doing nothing but recovering, you can afford to do that."

"Could we use the money to pay off our mortgage, or our home equity line of credit, as you call it?" asked Mel, ever the practical one.

"Anything. Once you've been diagnosed, the money is yours to spend as you like," I replied.

> *Dessanomics* integrates the relatively small expense of critical illness insurance into an efficient cash flow machine, so it becomes affordable. In my experience, as soon as clients see they can protect themselves and their families and still achieve their other financial goals, they enthusiastically welcome the protection critical life insurance provides.

"That sounds expensive," Mel said.

"Think about the odds," I said. And considering the odds, if you get sick, do you want to have to choose between cashing in your investments – and your retirement plans – and borrowing on the equity in your home? A critical insurance policy will give you tax-free money in your pocket. It will give you the peace of mind that comes from knowing you will be able to get the best medical care because you can afford it. You will be able to focus on getting better rather than worrying about your finances. How much is that worth to you?

"Think of critical illness insurance as retirement insurance, Mel – or, as I like to call it, quality-of-life insurance. It's one thing to make plans to achieve the retirement you want, but when does life ever unfold the way we expect it to? We also have to make sure your plan is protected. We're going to talk about protecting it from market downturns next, but first, we have to protect it from the loss of your income – permanently or temporarily."

Dessanomics KEY: 9

AN EXPERIENCED ADVISOR CAN HELP YOU BUY THE RIGHT KIND OF INSURANCE FOR YOU, IN THE RIGHT AMOUNT, AT THE RIGHT PRICE. YOU DESERVE THE PEACE OF MIND AND SECURITY, AND SO DOES YOUR FAMILY.

Chapter 6:

YES, MOLLY, YOU NEED TO INVEST IN THE STOCK MARKET, EVEN IN RETIREMENT, BUT YOU DON'T HAVE TO LOSE SLEEP

■ ■ ■

L et's begin by recapping the basics of portfolio construction. While this is a subject that can and has filled many long and largely unreadable books, I'm going to break it down very simply.

To meet your long-term investment goals, traditional wisdom says you need:

- Cash (or cash alternatives such as short-term GICs and bonds) for liquidity

> • Longer-term government bonds for guaranteed returns, bonds and dividend-paying stocks for income, and
>
> • Equities (stocks or funds that hold stocks) for growth

Until recently, traditional wisdom also said you didn't need growth once you'd reached retirement, so you didn't need equities past that point.

When my grandfather, Lazar Kaspardlov, retired in 1967, he was 68 years old. Life expectancy for women in Canada in 1970 was 73 years, less for men. A sudden stroke ended Papa's life shortly after he turned 69. His retirement lasted one year.

So much has changed in the four decades since my grandfather's death. By 1996, according to Statistics Canada, men could expect to live 78.6 years, and women 81.4 years. If a couple both reach age 65, at least one of them can now expect to live past age 90. Social status, physical exercise, strong social networks, a variety of interests and having a pet are just some of the things that may extend our life expectancy even further.

Combine those factors with the dream of many Canadians to retire at age 55 or 60, and it becomes clear that retirement can be expected to last for 20 or 30 years, or even longer.

We retire younger, we live longer, we're more active, and we are far healthier than ever before.

In other words, the traditional wisdom that worked for my grandfather's generation is completely, totally wrong for today's retirees. Today, retirees need growth in their portfolio as much at age 65 as they do at age 45.

Let's take a look at the Youngs as an example. Mel and Molly were educated and active. They had a dog and a cat, and were happily married and wealthy in a relative sense. (And of course, they would be a lot wealthier after embracing *Dessanomics!*) Molly's grandmother was 94, so we knew there was longevity in her family. Mel was adopted so we had no family history. It was likely that Molly would live to be 95, but what if she lived to 105?

Why in the world would Mel and Molly adopt a financial plan that left them with nothing at age 90? How do you pay medical expenses at age 95 with no money left? Yet that is exactly what would have resulted from the financial plan their former advisor had prepared.

With today's life expectancies, it's essential to assume you're going to live much longer than you think.

As I mentioned earlier, even RRIFs are set up to make sure you run out of money. After age 90, you're required to take out 20% each year. It doesn't take a mathematical genius to figure out that, at that rate your money won't last long.

LONGER LIVES, SMALLER DOLLARS

Now that we know you're going to need your money to last for 20, 30 or even 40 years after you receive your last pay cheque, it's time to consider inflation. Applying the rule of 72, we can quickly calculate that, even if inflation averages 3%, costs will double within 24 years. (The rule of 72 is simply 72 divided by the rate. In this case, the rate is 3%.)

It wasn't that long ago that I went to the corner store with a quarter to get a loaf of bread for my mother. I got the bread and a pocket full of candy that I enjoyed on the way home. I'm not that old, and when I thought about how long ago that was, I realized it was about the same amount of time I'd spend in retirement.

Here's something interesting about the inflation rate that you're probably not aware of: it is averaged across a large group of people. When broken down demographically to consider spending patterns, it is highest for retirees. When overall inflation is about 2.5% for the year, according to the Consumer Price Index-Elder (CPI-E), it is generally higher (about 3%) for those in retirement, because of the nature of retiree spending.

To ensure your money earns more than inflation takes away, we need to understand equity exposure.

Equity is your portion of ownership of companies represented by stocks, or by funds that invest in stocks. To be a successful equity investor, you should own great companies that have several things in common: they continue to grow their earnings and have superior management, free cash flow, hard assets and – most importantly – profits.

The reason you need to own great companies is it's the only way you can grow your capital (otherwise known as your money!).

Let me explain it this way. When you invest in a GIC or government bond, you lend your money to the bank (or bond issuer) for a specific period. During that period, they agree to pay you interest. (Think of it as rent on your money). At the end of the specified period, you get your capital back, along with your interest, minus inflation and taxes. (Corporate bonds work a bit differently, but you get the idea.)

How much did your original capital grow? Zippo! If you invested $10,000, you'd still have the original $10k. Over long periods that $10,000 has less and less value as inflation erodes its purchasing power.

Remember my example? Bread cost less than 25 cents a loaf 45 years ago, and about $3.50 today. That's a 1,400% increase in price. How much do you think that $10,000 will buy 30 or 40 years from now? Yes, the answer is – not much.

A well-chosen company stock, on the other hand, may pay you a dividend while you are waiting, similar to the interest you'd earn on a GIC or bond. And when the stock price increases, you have capital growth, which over the long term is the only means we know of to outpace inflation.

Once again, tax regulations play a role here. If you own your GIC or bond in a non-registered account (outside of your RRSP or RRIF), you will also have to pay the highest rate of tax on the interest earned (although you can squirrel away as much as $5,000 in a Tax Free Savings Account that grows tax-free.) In Ontario, for example, the top rate for 2008 is 46%. Dividend income is much more favourably taxed, at about 24%, and capital gains are taxed at about 23% (50% of the rate for employment or interest income).

So your best option is to have equity exposure. It's the only way to grow your capital and pay the least amount of tax possible.

That's a scary thought for many people at the moment, because we've just come through a period in which world markets have declined by between 25% and 70%, the Dow Jones Industrial Average had its biggest one-day loss in history, the housing market continues to sag, and people are still losing their homes and their jobs. Major market declines and contractions tend to happen about every five or six years, but human memory is funny. In bull markets, we forget that nothing goes up forever. And during declines, we forget that markets will recover and companies will still make profits. The only correction that seems to have any significance is the one we are in right at this very moment.

But remember this. While you're sitting on your hands wondering if you're going to have to learn how to pick berries in the woods or make dog food stew, Warren Buffet is spending billions of dollars on stocks (great companies!) even as I write. He understands that we need to look at the long term. You need your money to last for the long term. Remember how long you're going to live? Your savings will have to last 30 or 40 years, maybe longer.

Just imagine where you'd be if you had started to invest your money 50 years ago (assuming, of course, you were even alive then). If you'd invested just $100 a month over those 50 years, and managed average annual returns of even 7%, you'd be sitting on about $550,000 today, even though your total contributions would be less than $60,000. That's the magic of a compound interest, my friend, but it doesn't work as well without equity returns.

Let's try the same exercise using 2.5% as the average annual rate of return – about what you'd earn on a 10-year Government of Canada bond today. After 50 years, you'd have about $120,000, and a very different retirement lifestyle.

Dessanomics
KEY:
10

IN ORDER TO OUTPACE INFLATION, YOU NEED TO INCLUDE EQUITIES IN YOUR RETIREMENT PLAN, BUT YOU DON'T HAVE TO PUT YOUR SAVINGS AT RISK. WITH GUARANTEES, YOU CAN BUY AFFORDABLE INSURANCE PROTECTION FOR YOUR GREATEST ASSET – YOUR FUTURE.

MUTUAL FUNDS VERSUS SEGREGATED FUNDS

Average Canadians have two basic options when it comes to including equity in their portfolios: mutual funds and segregated funds. This, of course, is the point at which you will need an advisor who can help you determine which of the thousands of choices are right for you. (You can also invest in things called Exchange Traded Funds, but you need to know what you're doing.)

At this point in my conversation with Mel and Molly, she said, "I don't like mutual funds."

In my experience, people are usually afraid of the unknown, and many people have had bad experiences because they didn't do the necessary planning before they invested.

"Mutual funds are way too risky and expensive," said Molly. "Everyone always loses money in them. I've heard that from my friends at work a hundred times."

"That is what a lot of people think, Molly," I said. "And that's often their experience because they don't get the advice they need and therefore don't invest in the funds that are right for them."

In my experience, people have enough stress in their lives on a daily basis just raising their families and making a living. They don't need the additional burden of worrying about their futures – and they DO NOT want to end up like the employees of Enron.

"But let's put that aside for a minute and start with the basics. Do you know exactly what a mutual fund is? Or what a segregated fund is? There is no need to be embarrassed if you don't. A lot of people have no more than a vague idea, and that's part of the reason that many people have lost money."

"I think that accurately describes us," said Molly.

"Okay, then," I said. "Mutual funds are a pool of investments that you and a bunch of other people buy. They offer professional management and diversification across asset classes, management styles, geographic location and size and type of company."

Diversification is absolutely essential, I told Mel and Molly, but it is really time-consuming and expensive to try to achieve it by investing yourself directly in stocks.

Diversification and professional management greatly reduce market risk. But markets will always go up and down, and so will mutual funds. That's why their returns aren't guaranteed the way GICs are.

Segregated funds are guaranteed. They are essentially mutual funds that include a guarantee that you will get your principle (the amount you invested) back at a certain date no matter what happens in the market.

"Guaranteed! There is no such thing as a guaranteed mutual fund," said Mel. "Everyone knows that."

"Yes, I know. It's true that mutual funds aren't guaranteed, but segregated funds are. A seg fund is a mutual fund with an insurance wrapper around it, like a blanket to keep it safe and warm," I said.

With seg funds, you pay a premium to transfer the market risk to the insurance company. In return, you give yourself some peace of mind. As we discussed, it is essential to have equity exposure in order to grow your capital and reduce your taxes, but the ups and downs of the market are just too much for a lot of people. These guarantees will help keep your emotions out of your decisions. In my experience, people generally make very bad decisions when they are financially stressed.

Many of Canada's greatest mutual funds are available in both forms. You can buy the naked mutual fund, or you can buy the mutual fund inside a segregated fund (the same fund, insured and guaranteed).

> Raised by one parent who served in WWII and the other born in the Great Depression, I favoured an investing strategy that closely hugged a safe and guaranteed return type of path. My wife comes from a similar background, so Dessa and her very capable team faced some big obstacles in encouraging us to explore some alternative investment options that could improve the overall value of our portfolio. While respecting our conservative investing roots, *Dessanomics* uncovered unique options that offer both greater return potential and the relatively safe configuration that makes us comfortable. This process has guided us into an appropriate financial home makeover without tearing down walls.

THE OVERLY CAUTIOUS WWII VETERAN'S SON & HIS ACCOUNTANT WIFE

Seg funds are more expensive, of course, but as usual, you get what you pay for.

Let me tell you the real deal regarding the cost. At time of writing, the long-term rate of return for one of Canada's most popular asset allocation funds was about 10% since inception about

11 years ago. If you invested in the fund over 11 years, you'd have an average annual return of 10%. However, you would also have had to live with some steep declines and the worry that your hard-earned money – or at least a good portion of it – wouldn't be there when you needed it. Not everyone can handle that anxiety, and too many people end up taking a loss just to stop the worry.

However, if you bought the same fund insured by one of the great insurance companies, your rate of return would be about 9.5%, somewhere between 0.25% and 0.75% less than the mutual fund itself, to cover off the cost of insurance. But your investment would be guaranteed. Some seg funds will cost slightly more and some slightly less. It really depends on the bells and whistles you choose to include.

For that relatively small cost, as of the writing of this book, this is what you get from a seg fund:

1. Up to 100% guarantee on your capital. In other words, your money is insured. (It could be as low as a guarantee of 75% of your capital depending on the options you choose.)

2. A death benefit of 100% or more. If you die during the agreed term, some segregated funds will provide a benefit to your heirs equal to your invested capital plus returns.

3. The ability to bypass probate on death. The money goes directly to your named beneficiary and does not become part of your estate, saving thousands of dollars in probate fees. In Ontario, for example, an estate of $500,000 would cost $7,000 to probate. Wouldn't you rather leave that money to people you love?

4. By law, insurance companies must settle with your heirs within 30 days, saving your executors time and money. And they do!

5. Commissions and fees are usually waived on death.

6. Creditor protection. If you are sued, your adversary cannot get his hands on your money, a very important benefit, particularly for those who are professional or self-employed or who travel in more litigious environments.

7. Segregated funds keep your wealth private. Did you know that when you die, your will becomes a public document? Anyone can get a copy. Anyone! Seg funds, on the other hand, become the property of the beneficiary, so they're private.

8. In some cases, seg funds provide the opportunity to lock in your market gains or reset the amount of your guarantee to the new, higher value.

9. Seg funds give you access to the most tax-efficient income in the marketplace today (in non-registered investments).

For many people, the benefits alone are well worth the price of admission, but I've saved the best for last. (And so have the insurance companies. The benefit I'm about to describe has only recently become available in Canada.)

GMWB: YOUR NEW BFF

BFF: That's Best Friend Forever, for you non-techies.

Seg funds come with Guaranteed Minimum Withdrawal Benefits (GMWBs), which I mentioned a while ago, and that provides a guaranteed income alternative for those who do not have access to an employer pension. They provide income for life – guaranteed! You will have income for life, with the added benefit of having liquidity. Your money is not locked in, and you can get at it if you want to. GMWBs offer all the flexibility of a mutual fund account, but without the market risk!

I believe the most important feature of a GMWB is the ability to guarantee the lifetime annual income amount.

In addition to the seg fund benefits noted previously, GMWB products can provide additional benefits as of December 2008:

1. The opportunity to get a minimum 5% bonus in every year that you continue to acquire assets, or are not taking income, so that your guaranteed minimum payout is increasing a minimum of 5% per year, even when the markets are in the red.

2. In addition to the usual reset options available on some seg funds, GMWB products give you the best of both worlds. If the market value of your fund goes down during the year, you will receive the 5% bonus. If the market value of your fund goes up more than 5%, you will receive the higher value. The very worst thing that can happen is you will get back – in the form of income – your original deposits, plus the 5% per year bonus for every year you do not take income.

GMWBs are the only products in the marketplace today that will give you predictable (guaranteed not to decrease), sustainable (guaranteed for your lifetime) income – with the potential for growth. Previously, the only way to get guaranteed lifetime income was to purchase a life annuity, and unfortunately, that meant losing access to your capital and any flexibility or potential for growth. An annuity may still be an option, especially for Molly's LIRA money, but that is still at least 16 years away.

In my opinion, GMWBs are everything good all rolled into one: the security of a GIC, the income stream of an annuity or pension, and the potential upside of the market.

> With a GMWB, my clients know their income has a floor - a minimum that it will not go below no matter how bad markets are. This protection gives them peace of mind and certainty. There is no other product on the market today that provides flexibility and market participation.

The aim of investing used to be all about having the correct asset allocation, and it continues to be true that we need a variety of stocks and bonds in our underlying investments. But today, it is most important to make sure we have the right product allocation, and that we have the products that will provide our own personal pension plan if we don't have an adequate employer pension.

For people like Mel and Molly, whose tiny pension will not sustain them, and for anyone who wants to ensure that their RRIF income will not be affected by early market volatility, GMWBs are the place to look.

So let me ask you. Which fund do you want? The Canadian asset allocation with the long-term rate of return of 10.5%? Or the same fund in a seg package with all the benefits I just talked about, and a slightly lower rate of return?

Remember – guaranteed income for life, versus watching the value of your money go up for a while and then plummet with the market.

For most of my clients who value a good night's sleep over that extra 0.25 to 0.75% return, it's a no-brainer. You really do get what you pay for.

It is amazing how much quality of life improves when people know exactly how much income they can expect when they retire. Until recently, advisors could only estimate – and most did not worry about sequence of returns until it was too late and their retired clients had lost much of their spending power. (Sequence of return risk refers to the fact that a substantial loss early in retirement has devastating consequences, as there is no additional income or time with which to rebuild capital.)

I believe the most important feature of a GMWB is the ability to guarantee the lifetime monthly income amount.

Chapter 7:

PUTTING IT ALL TOGETHER – *DESSANOMICS* IN ACTION

■ ■ ■

After our meeting, Mel and Molly left my office to meet Hank and Linda for dinner at their favourite restaurant. They'd been eating there for years. In fact, it was the restaurant where Mel and Molly got engaged.

"Well," said Hank, "how did your first meeting go with Dessa?"

"I'll bet your heads are spinning," said Linda, with a big smile.

"You know, I never thought in a million years that we could cover so many things in two hours," said Mel. "I'll definitely need time to digest everything we went over, and I'm still not entirely sure how we're going to accomplish everything she talked about. I have to admit I feel a bit overwhelmed. But one thing I know for sure is that I know a lot more than I did three hours ago!"

"The thing that surprises me the most," said Molly, "is how much this process has changed the way we manage debt. For example, our mortgage. I guess I shouldn't be too surprised that our bank isn't going to teach us how to pay it less interest, but I'm amazed that nobody seems to know about this stuff except perhaps you two!"

Hank and Linda laughed and looked at each other – it must be said – a little smugly.

"I did the budget sheet Dessa requested, but she had actually gone over our bank statements for the past six months," said Molly. "I guess she wants to make sure she has the numbers right. There were so many things I'd never given much thought to. She kept adding to our lifestyle expenses: a new roof, provisions for Jo Layne's and Cori's weddings. I mean, Cori doesn't even have a boyfriend yet, and we're sure hoping Jo Layne isn't too serious about her current boyfriend."

They all laughed.

"The thing that really ticks me off," said Mel, "is how many books and newspaper articles I've read over the years that focused entirely on the things that we've been doing – and doing religiously – while never really getting ahead. I mean, we made the extra mortgage payments. We put money into RRSPs every year. We keep a rainy day account with three months of expenses in it.

"Even though we make a good living and aren't big spenders by any means, we never would have been able to save enough for retirement on the track we were on.

"But I'm still unclear how all this is supposed to work out. I understand that rolling our personal line of credit into a lower-interest home equity line of credit will save us some money on interest. Depositing our RRSP contributions monthly instead of at the last minute in February is clearly a good idea. But that doesn't add up to the kind of money I think we're going to need. This all seems like a lot of work to save a few hundred bucks in interest or make a few hundred extra on my RRSP."

"But that's just one small part of *Dessanomics*," said Hank. "When Linda and I first went through the process, it was a lot of work. You know how disorganized we are. We had to go to so many meetings before Dessa could complete that plan. We had three different lines of credit, and so many credit cards I couldn't count them all. There were even some I didn't know about – right, honey?" he said, winking at Linda.

Linda replied, "Well, every time I went to the store to get something for the kids, the cashier would say, 'If you sign up for our store credit card you will save another 20%.' So I did. I was working hard to save you money, dear."

"Yeah, okay," said Hank. "We'll blame that one on the kids. On top of all that, and our mortgage, we also owed money to Linda's father for the down payment on our first house. We didn't have a set payment plan, or a time frame to pay it back, but Dessa dug down deep and figured out a way to get the money back to Linda's parents in a more timely manner.

"You know, it's funny, but when we finally had a plan to pay them off, you would not believe how much better we felt, how much more in control of our lives. It was like we were finally grown-ups. Their retirement is important, too. We were able to pay them off, and today we have a plan to help our kids when it's time for them to buy a home. Hopefully it won't be too soon, as we both want them to finish school first. But when they're ready, all we have to do is write a cheque. You would not believe how good we feel about being in control of all that. The greatest thing about having our finances in order isn't the money – it's the way we feel," said Hank.

"You are such a control freak!" said Linda, laughing.

"Hey, I'm a control freak so you can enjoy being artistic remember," said Hank in his own defence. It was pretty clear these two had learned to love each other's differences when it came to money – which is what can happen once you have an effective plan in place to take care of the challenges.

"Molly, do you remember all the time we spent around the kitchen table talking about building our dream house? We spent so many hours going back and forth – not to mention the number of times we had to ask the architect to revise the plans before we finally felt we had it right," said Hank. "Back then, it seemed like we'd wasted a lot of time getting started, but all that extra work saved us so much time and money in the end. Our contractor said it was one of the smoothest projects he'd ever been on, because we'd done so much planning before we started building. That's the way we think about our work with Dessa, too. I really feel sorry for people who are trying to do this on their own or with an advisor they don't trust to work hard in their best interest."

"Dessa has reminded us a couple of times that most people spend more time planning their vacation or buying a car than they do on their personal finances," said Linda.

"I hear you," said Mel. "But I am still concerned about where she thinks she's going to get all this money to do everything she plans. To top it off, our insurance costs are going to go up because Dessa told us we were not adequately insured, either."

"We felt exactly the same way," said Hank. "Remember, things were even bleaker for us when we first met Dessa. You guys are doing great compared to where we were then! But the other thing you probably want to keep in mind is this. You already know that if you keep doing what you are doing, you're not going to be retired very long if you ever get there at all. Or you'll be one of those guys who spends all day lying in front of the TV because you can't afford anything else with the heat turned off to save money!

> When I was first introduced to *Dessanomics*, I already had what I thought was a plan. I had a nice nest egg of money saved, had just made the last payment on my car loan, and was now going to tackle paying down my credit-card debt. After a very lengthy discussion about how to deal with debt, I soon realized my plan made no sense. Because, if you have debt, you don't have savings. *Dessanomics* changed my situation within months. I applied the formula, and I'm now on my way to the retirement I wanted! Thank you *Dessanomics*!
>
> **THE BY-LAW ENFORCEMENT OFFICER**

"When Linda and I retire, we're going to spend our winters in Florida playing golf. It isn't a dream anymore – it's our future. We can't wait! I know exactly what the worst case scenario is, GUARANTEED. That's the reason we pushed you to see Dessa. Who am I going to golf with down there while you're up here working? It will be a very long winter without you to beat."

Molly was beginning to droop. An early morning, a long day and two hours of head spinning, personal finance information had worn her out. She signalled for the bill, and as had been their tradition for more than 30 years, Mel and Hank insisted on flipping a coin to decide who would pay.

"So when is your next meeting?" asked Hank on the way out the door.

"Thursday the 17th," said Mel. "I can't wait to see how Dessa can make our income stretch to fit that wish list – and still leave us a couple of vacations."

Chapter 8:

WORKING THE PLAN

■ ■ ■

Armed with my plan, I was ready for Mel and Molly. Like so many presentations before, I was really excited to show them what they could accomplish. They didn't know it yet, but their life was about to change – radically – for the better.

But when they sat down in my boardroom, the first thing that came out of Mel's mouth was, "Well, I guess I should have called you and let you know, but the company just cut our overtime. I'm sure this is going to screw up all of our plans. We understand you might have to go back and revise the plan. I'm really sorry that I didn't call to let you know, but it just didn't occur to me until this morning."

"Ouch, I'm sorry to hear that, Mel. That must be a disappointment for you. How much of a difference will it make in your income?" I asked.

"Last year, I made $170,000 plus the $10,000 from the fire department, which is why I was able to make a bigger RRSP contribution than I normally do. But my income will most likely go down to about $130,000 in total this year," he said.

"Not to worry, Mel. That might make a difference in your lifestyle, but not in our planning. I always work with the worst case scenario," I said.

Mel and Molly looked at each other with relief and settled back into their chairs. I could tell they'd had a difficult week, and it made me feel even happier to show them what was in store.

"Let's look at your current cash flow first, so you are completely clear on what your expenses are on a monthly basis. I have separated out your living expenses, because we're not going to touch them. We will talk about your income later," I said.

$1,100	$125,000 mortgage, 16 years at 6.5%
$350	$18,000 line of credit, 5 years at 7.5%
$250	$4,500 credit card at 18%
$600	Savings at year-end, 50% to RRSP, 50% to savings
$150	RRSP monthly contributions
$115	Life insurance, $150,000 each, 20 year term
$0	Critical Illness Insurance
$2,565	Expense total
$5,500	Lifestyle expenses
$8,065	Sub total
(-$205)	Less tax refund of $450 X 46%*
$7,860	Net after tax total

*$150/month RSP + $300/m (from 50% of annual savings)

"Pay special attention to these two numbers: your expenses (not including living expenses) are $2,565 each month, and your tax refund, averaged out over the year, is $205 per month. This is exactly (within the nearest five dollars) what your monthly expenses are now. You'll notice I've rounded off your living expenses and averaged them over the year. I've divided things like car insurance and vacations that you pay for once a year into 12, so everything is here.

"But that won't be a big part of our discussion. You two obviously know how to run a household budget, or you wouldn't have done nearly as well as you have. I've based all these figures on your past spending, averaged over time, so I know they're accurate. I'm here to help you make the most of the money you don't need for living expenses, not to tell you if you can go out for lunch or not," I said. "Now, let's go through the steps we need to take to make this engine run for you."

1. First, we're going to set up an all-in-one line of credit, the HELOC. These accounts aren't available to everyone. You need to have solid credit, a good income history and at least 20% equity in your home. That means the two of you will have no problem qualifying, and you're going to be amazed at the money it will make you.

   So, all of your debt and savings go into one big account. We will apply for this line of credit using your house as the collateral. As we discussed in our first meeting, we can apply for a maximum of 80% of the market value of your home. If your home is worth $300,000, your line of credit will be $240,000.

2. Then we are going to pay off your current mortgage, and all of your other debts.

3. Next, we will cash in your so-called savings and reduce your line of credit balance.

Mel threw back his head and put his hands over his face. "Our savings! Dessa, we have that money set aside for emergencies. Isn't that what we're supposed to do? It makes me feel sick to think we won't have that money to rely on if things go off the rails."

"Mel, I'm going to have to ask you to be patient and listen for a while. Trust me. I'm not going to push you into anything you're not comfortable with, but let's get the whole picture first, okay?"

"Alright," he said. "I'm sorry. It's just so different than what we've been told all our lives. It's going to take some time to get used to."

"That's why this process is so important, Mel. People aren't getting ahead doing what they've been told all their lives," I said.

Let's review the numbers. By removing the house and investments, you can clearly see how much debt you have:

Mel and Molly have:

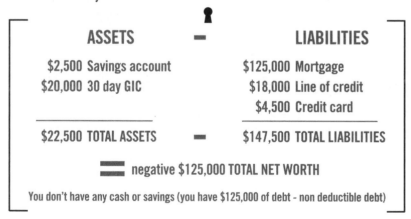

ASSETS	=	LIABILITIES
$2,500 Savings account		$125,000 Mortgage
$20,000 30 day GIC		$18,000 Line of credit
		$4,500 Credit card
$22,500 TOTAL ASSETS	=	$147,500 TOTAL LIABILITIES

= negative $125,000 TOTAL NET WORTH

You don't have any cash or savings (you have $125,000 of debt - non deductible debt)

This is what it should look like...

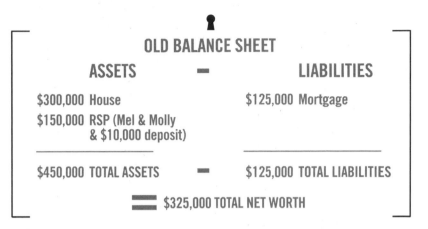

OLD BALANCE SHEET

ASSETS	**—**	LIABILITIES
$300,000 House		$125,000 Mortgage
$150,000 RSP (Mel & Molly & $10,000 deposit)		
$450,000 TOTAL ASSETS **—**		$125,000 TOTAL LIABILITIES
≡ $325,000 TOTAL NET WORTH		

"However, we are also going to borrow the $50,000 to top up your RRSP, and when you receive the refund of $27,600, we will use it to repay the loan balance. So the new liability balance will then be $147,400.

"Now, remember the balance sheet. We added $22,400 to the debt column, but we also added $50,000 to the assets column. All we had to do was move some numbers around so you could get YOUR money back from the government. All $27,600 worth! (That's a tax refund of 46% of $60,000.) I don't want to even think how big that number will be five or 10 years from now," I said.

NEW BALANCE SHEET

| ASSETS | — | LIABILITIES |

ASSETS — **LIABILITIES**

$300,000 House
$150,000 RSP (Mel & Molly
& $10,000 deposit)
$50,000 RSP top up deposit

$125,000 Mortgage
$50,000 RSP top up loan
-$27,600 Less refund

$500,000 TOTAL ASSETS — $147,400 TOTAL LIABILITIES

$352,600 TOTAL NET WORTH

Note the immediate increase of $27,600

"Now this is the part you're going to love – even more than adding $27,600 to your asset net worth without a single day's extra work. Your new line of credit will be at the bank's low lending rate, currently at 3.25%. But I'm going to do our calculations using 4%, which is closer to the long-term average. So, in addition to increasing your net worth, you're reducing your monthly debt payments.

"This is what your cash flow will look like. Remember all those suggestions I made that you thought you couldn't afford? I'm leaving your lifestyle expenses out, because that isn't part of this discussion," I said.

GROSS CASH FLOW

TRADITIONAL WAY   VS   *DESSANOMICS** WAY

TRADITIONAL WAY	DESSANOMICS* WAY
$1,100/m Mortgage	$490/m All-in-one line of credit - interest only $147,000 @ 4%
$350/m Line of credit	
$250/m Credit card	$1,200/m Increase RSP
$150/m RSP (pac)	$460/m Leverage investment
$600/m Savings	$85/m New life insurance $450,000 Mel & $150,00 Molly
$115/m Life insurance $150,000 @ Mel & Molly	
$0/m Critical Illness Insurance	$130/m Critical illness $100,000 each Mel/Molly
$2,565 TOTAL	$2,365 TOTAL

*New HELOC will be: $125,000 + $50,000
(RSP deposit) less refund of
$60,000 @ 46% ($27,600)

$125,000
- $50,000
($27,600)
$147,400

"Whoa," said Mel. "That's less than we were paying before, which is great. But how are we going to pay off the line of credit if we only make interest payments? I don't want to retire with a huge debt hanging over our heads."

"Yes, but we're not done yet, Mel," I said. We need to add another line, because the tax refunds still need to be deducted. Remember your RRSP tax refund of $205 each month? This is what it looks like now."

NET AFTER TAX CASH REQUIREMENTS

TRADITIONAL WAY   VS   *DESSANOMICS* WAY

TRADITIONAL WAY	DESSANOMICS WAY
$2,565	$2,365
($205) Less refund ($450 @ 46%)	($760) Less refund ($1,200 + $460 @ 46%)
$2,360	$1,605

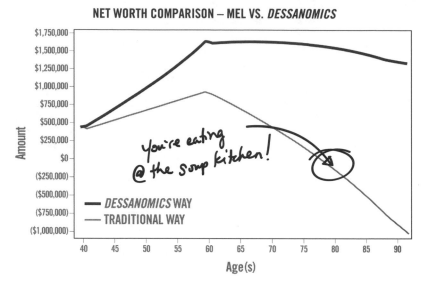

NET WORTH COMPARISON – MEL VS. *DESSANOMICS*

"So, your new after-tax net monthly cash requirement, minus living expenses, is just $1,605," I said.

"Okay, I get it," said Mel. "That's $755 per month less than we are currently paying. But if we use the tax refund to pay off the principal balance on the line of credit, if I'm figuring correctly, it's going to take us about the same amount of time to pay off as in our earlier plan – not the 10 years that Molly figured out in our first meeting," said Mel.

"Your math is correct – but it's important to look at the whole picture," I said. "We're still not finished."

"First, let's look at the difference this will make to your RRSP. If you continued on the path you were on when we first met, it would grow to less than $675,000. That's clearly not enough to maintain your lifestyle, and that assumes your average annual returns are 8%, which sure isn't guaranteed. We could set up a guaranteed minimum withdrawal benefit, which would guarantee 5% per year.

That would only leave you with $390,000 at retirement, but at least you could sleep well at night knowing it was guaranteed.

Some of the best leverage candidates are those individuals who have pensions. These people (because of pension adjustments) have little RRSP room annually, so they have few options to reduce their tax burden. Leveraging gives them the perfect opportunity to gain superior wealth and reduce taxes, today and in the future.

This group includes teachers, police officers, health care workers and many others who work for the government. This group has guaranteed income; their jobs are secure and so are their pensions, so they can – all else being equal – often afford to take on greater leverage risk.

But in fact, this group of people have a tendency to be the most risk-averse. If you happen to be in this situation, I urge you to give some thought to the way this part of the *Dessanomics* plan would enhance your wealth creation.

"Now let's look at my numbers. This is what your situation will look like when you're 65 with the *Dessanomics* plan. We're going to look at the worst case scenario first. This assumes we get no growth, and your only increase is the 5% annual bonus within the GMWB."

I continued with Mel and Molly.

"Your RRSP guarantee will be $716,000.
Your leverage investment guarantee will be $190,000.
AND because of the way we've paid off your home equity line of credit, you will have a cash account with over $385,000.

When debt service ratios fit, I recommend that my clients invest in one of two types of investments: either a GMWB, as with the Youngs, or a regular segregated fund. It is essential that my clients be able to sleep at night when the markets go in the ash can. Using this type of investment is what personal finance author Talbot Stevens calls "conservative leverage," and it is a much different proposition than simply gambling on the markets with borrowed money. I have found over the years that my clients are very happy to give up some of the profits on the upside to the insurance company to have that protection on the downside.

"We still have to pay back $100,000 to the bank to pay off your leverage line of credit, so your total minimum retirement fund will be $1,191,000.

$716,000 + $ 190,000 + $385,000 minus $100,000 = $1,191,000

"So, not to put too fine a point on it, Mel, but we've increased your minimum pension pool by more than $800,000 while using less of your monthly income. Plus we've removed the market risk, all by changing your cash flow strategy. And remember, with your plan, you would have been bust by about 85."

Mel couldn't hide the smile on his face. "Tell us how much we'll have if our average returns are 8%? I mean, the great thing about making these changes now is that we're ramping up our investments at what must be pretty close to a market bottom, right?"

"One of the reasons we're making these changes is so you don't have to count on the market – not even Warren Buffett can time the market – but it's pretty safe to assume that this is a better time to ramp up your investment than any other time in the last 10 years," I said.

Here's how things would turn out with an 8% average annual return over the same period:

The RRSP will be $1,056,000
The leverage investment will be $337,000
And the cash account will be the same, $385,000
(Less the bank loan of $100,000)

For a TOTAL of $1,722,000

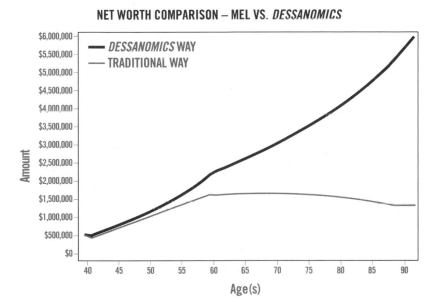

NET WORTH COMPARISON – MEL VS. *DESSANOMICS*

There was dead silence around the table. While Mel and Molly wrapped their heads around their new future, I went to find some fresh coffee. Caffeine would help us all stay sharp for the next round.

Still not convinced that *Dessanomics* works? Here are three more examples of the process in action. These charts represent the changes we were able to make with clients at three different levels of financial commitment.
Isn't it time your personal wealth went the *Dessanomics* way?

NET WORTH COMPARISON – LOW

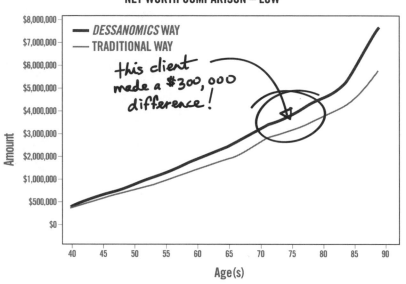

NET WORTH COMPARISON – AVERAGE

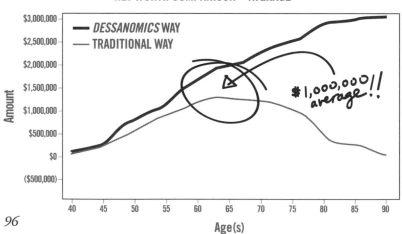

NET WORTH COMPARISON – HIGH

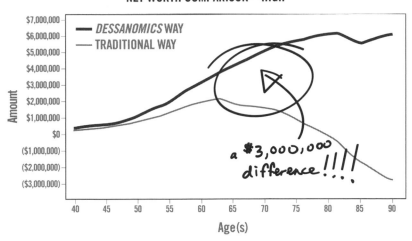

Many of my clients prefer to not use their home as collateral for their leverage investments, and I understand their position. The argument that this is less expensive is not always true. Today, as an example, the rate on home equity lending is at 3.5%; the rate on non home equity lending is 3%.

Chapter 9:

RETIRING THE MORTGAGE

■ ■ ■

Both Mel and Molly were looking a little stunned when I came back in with the coffee, so I took some time to walk them through the charts and calculations that I'd made.

"There's no question I'm impressed, Dessa," said Mel after looking carefully through my calculations. (Molly seemed to have been struck dumb, but she looked very happy.)

"You've showed us how to make almost an extra million dollars using less of our monthly income. You haven't asked us to change our lifestyle or give up our vacations. I didn't think it was possible. But we still haven't paid off the house, and that's always been our number one goal – to be mortgage-free before we retire."

Mel was a tough cookie, and he wasn't going down easy. He wanted to be sure he had every angle covered, and rightly so. But I wasn't worried. This was familiar territory for me.

Cash Inflows	YEAR 5	YEAR 6	YEAR 7	YEAR 8	YEAR 9	YEAR 10
Employment Inflows:						
Employment Salary (Mel)	104,335	107,465	110,689	114,009	117,430	120,952
Volunteer Fireman Income (Mel)	10,000	10,000	10,000	10,000	10,000	10,000
Employment Salary (Molly)	34,778	35,822	36,896	38,003	39,143	40,317
Total Employment Inflows:	**149,113**	**153,286**	**157,585**	**162,012**	**166,573**	**171,270**
Investment Inflows:						
Mel's Leverage Investment (Non-Reg.)	8,163	8,816	9,521	10,283	11,106	11,994
Return on Surplus Funds (Joint)	0	0	0	549	1,328	2,149
Total Investment Inflows:	**8,163**	**8,816**	**9,521**	**10,831**	**12,433**	**14,143**
Total Cash Inflows:	**157,276**	**162,102**	**167,106**	**172,844**	**179,006**	**185,413**
Cash Outflows						
Lifestyle Expenses:						
Lifestyle Expense (Mel)	63,760	65,673	67,643	69,672	71,763	73,915
Mortgage (Joint)	27,764	28,780	7,827	0	0	0
Total Lifestyles Expenses:	**91,524**	**94,453**	**75,470**	**69,672**	**71,763**	**73,915**
Employment/Business Expenses:						
Employment Insurance Premiums (Mel)	860	886	912	939	968	997
Employment Insurance Premiums (Molly)	626	645	664	684	705	726
Total Employment/Business Expenses:	**1,486**	**1,530**	**1,576**	**1,623**	**1,672**	**1,722**
Non-Registered Contributions & Reinvestments:						
Mel's Leverage Investment (Non-Reg.)	8,163	8,816	9,521	10,283	11,106	11,994
Total Non-Registered Contributions & Reinvestments:	**8,163**	**8,816**	**9,521**	**10,283**	**11,106**	**11,994**
Investment Expenses:						
Untitled Leverage Liability (Mel)	5,250	5,250	5,250	5,250	5,250	5,250
Cost on Deficit Funds (Joint)	0	0	0	0	0	0
Total Investment Expenses:	**5,250**	**5,250**	**5,250**	**5,250**	**5,250**	**5,250**
Registered Contributions:						
CPP/QPP Contrib. - Employment (Mel)	2,410	2,487	2,567	2,649	2,734	2,821
Mel's RSP (RRSP)	14,400	14,400	14,400	14,400	14,400	14,400
CPP/QPP Contrib. - Employment (Molly)	1,548	1,600	1,653	1,708	1,764	1,822
Total Registered Contributions:	**18,358**	**18,487**	**18,620**	**18,757**	**18,898**	**19,044**
Miscellaneous Expenses:						
Life Insurance (Mel)	1,020	1,020	1,020	1,020	1,020	1,020
Medical Coverage Plan (Mel)	1,560	1,560	1,560	1,560	1,560	1,560
Total Miscellaneous Expenses:	**2,580**	**2,580**	**2,580**	**2,580**	**2,580**	**2,580**
Taxes:						
Net Federal Tax (Mel)	16,643	17,264	17,908	18,574	19,268	19,988
Net Provincial Tax (Mel)	8,615	8,934	9,266	9,611	9,971	10,345
Net Federal Tax (Molly)	3,075	3,167	3,261	3,443	3,662	3,891
Net Provincial Tax (Molly)	1,582	1,621	1,714	1,884	1,972	2,064
Total Taxes:	**29,916**	**30,986**	**32,149**	**33,512**	**34,873**	**36,288**
Total Cash Outflows:	**157,276**	**162,102**	**145,166**	**141,678**	**146,142**	**150,793**
Current Surplus/(Deficit)	0	0	21,940	31,166	32,864	34,620
Previous Surplus/(Deficit)	0	0	0	21,940	53,106	85,971
Ending Surplus/(Deficit)	0	0	21,940	53,106	85,971	120,591

*Note: Income expenses have been increased annually by the inflation rate of 3%.

mortge free!

building a real rainy day accou

"I've been saving this for last, because I think you're both going to love it," I said. "Once we make the changes to your cash flow structure, and we apply the money you're saving to your HELOC principal, look what happens. Yep! Your non-deductible debt is paid off in seven years – less than half the time you'd planned. Can you imagine how good that is going to feel?"

"Seven years! That's unbelievable," said Mel. "But surely this will all change with my cut in overtime pay. I suppose that will throw a monkey wrench into things."

"No, take a look at the top line in your cash flow chart. I've used total income of $130,000 per year: $100,000 for you and $30,000 for Molly. Again, I wanted to show you the worst case scenario, and I knew that your overtime would not be consistent over the next 16 years. Your industry is like most – it goes through cycles, so it is important that we build that into our plan."

> Two years ago, I sought financial advice from Dessa and her team for myself and my brother, who has failing health. I'm a 61-year old retired teacher, and the only recommendation the others offered was a "one-size-fits-all" portfolio. Using *Dessanomics*, we were able to develop a specific plan that met both my brother's unique needs and my own plans for long-term investment strategies. I have the utmost confidence in *Dessanomics* – this process has truly lifted a tremendous burden off my shoulders.
>
> **THE SINGLE RETIRED TEACHER**

"Can you explain again how we're going to pay off the home equity line of credit in seven years? I just can't figure out how that's going to work," said Molly.

"It's all about applying your cash flow efficiently," I said. "Remember, the first thing we do is reduce the amount of income tax and interest you're paying, and we apply the cash you've got in low interest, taxable GICs and savings to your debt. With no money sitting around generating new tax bills while you have debts that carry interest charges, every penny will be put to use, just as soon as your pay cheque hits the bank.

There is a story I like to tell my clients that I think puts leverage in perspective. In Dunfermline, Scotland, in 1835, a boy was born to a working-class family. Soon after, his father lost his job and the family emigrated to the United States. They settled in Pittsburgh, and in 1848, the boy's father died. To help feed his family, as well as himself, he went to work as a bobbin boy in a textile mill. He was 13 years old. Over the next eight years, he had several jobs – enough to figure out that he was capable of more, and didn't want to work for a wage all of his life. At the age of 21, he borrowed a little more than $200 from his friendly banker. (I really don't know if the banker was friendly or not, but I find the irony makes people smile.) That's about $80,000 in today's dollars, a mighty sum for a 21- year-old. He invested in the Woodruff Sleeping Car Company, and within two years, his investment was earning him about $5,000 each year, equivalent to about $1,500,000 today.

The boy's name was Andrew Carnegie, and I believe you know the rest of the story. But what most people don't know about Andrew Carnegie is that we never would have heard of him were it not for his willingness to use other people's money to leverage his fortune. There is no question that there are risks associated with leverage, but in my mind, they are not nearly as great as the risks associated with NOT leveraging.

"Every time you reduce your loan balance, it also reduces your interest cost – and these savings in turn will help to pay down the balance. Think of it as a big money-recycling plant that helps you squeeze every ounce of efficiency out of your money. When you look at the effect over days, weeks, months and years, it really adds up fast.

"On top of that," I continued, "you're now making much larger monthly RRSP contributions, which will save you more income tax. The government is willing to help you save for retirement, but you weren't taking full advantage of that before, and now you can. Then we added leverage – letting other people's money help you prepare for retirement – using a GMWB and a no-margin-call loan to reduce your risk (a no-margin-call loan is usually only available from the company that holds your investments. A conventional bank may not provide this.) Because the interest on that line of credit is tax-deductible, it reduces your income tax even more in addition to giving you a large pool of money to put to work for you. Even if market returns are poor, you will be able to count on the annual bonus until you are ready to retire and draw income."

"It's all about efficiency," I continued. "By changing the way you manage your cash flow, we've made your income much more tax-efficient now. We don't have to go into how you will draw income in retirement yet, but if you want an idea of what tax efficiency will look like then, take a look at this chart."

There are several ways that investment loans can be arranged. I've referred to the method that worked best for Mel and Molly. I encourage you to speak to your advisor about the strategies and products that will work best for your individual situation.

THE RETIREMENT PURSE

"Now, you said you wanted income of $75,000 each year, and because I know you mean the equivalent of $75,000 in today's dollars, we need to inflate that figure so you have $75,000 in actual spending power.

"At 3% inflation, you will need about $120,000 per year when you're ready to retire. If you look at my WORST case scenario, when we combine CPP, OAS and the GMWB from your RRSP, LIRA and leveraged investment account, the minimum guaranteed amount in the first year will be $83,000.

"So you can see pretty clearly that if you had continued on the plan you were on, you'd need to stock up on a lot of macaroni and cheese dinners. Even this worst case scenario is a little short of your goal, but remember, we're assuming that your income is cut from now until retirement and that, over the next 16 years, the stock market never makes any money. Based on where the markets are today, I believe that scenario is most unlikely," I said.

"Now let's look at what happens if your income never increases, but we get reasonable profits from the markets. Your income in that first year would then be – guaranteed – just over $120,000 year. These are both only estimates, and your income in retirement will probably be somewhere between the two, but you can see that your range is now somewhere between $86,000 and $120,000. Whatever happens, you can retire when you want to, and you can have the kind of lifestyle you want. Using a GMWB, we can also guarantee your income for life – your own personal pension plan."

"I love that idea," said Molly. "The more I think about it, the more I like knowing that we'll be able to count on our income. I've known so many people who spent too much of their retirement wondering if their investments would hold up, and I'm just so relieved we won't have to do that."

> With *Dessanomics*, we know that our carefully built investments are well protected even in today's economy, and that helps us get comfortable with retirement.
>
> THE NURSE & THE INDEPENDENT BUSINESSMAN

"That's the reason I call this your personal pension plan," I said. "The days of being employed by one company for life and then being looked after by that company's pension plan in retirement are gone. But with these new products, you can have the same kind of security. You will know what the minimum guaranteed income is for life, and you're right, other investments sure can't promise that."

There are some differences, though, as I explained to Mel and Molly. A pension plan won't give you an extra payment here and there when you need it, but a GMWB can. If you need extra money, you can always redeem some of your account balance just as you can with any other investment.

And unlike a pension, or even an annuity, whatever is left in your GMWB when you die will go to your beneficiaries.

"So, it's like a pension – only better," said Molly.

"Yes, exactly," I replied. "I'm convinced that once everyone understands the benefits of these products, there is no way Canadians will be willing to roll the dice on regular mutual funds and stocks."

"Now, before we finish today," I continued, "I want to go over one more strategy, because even though the interest is tax-deductible, we'll want to pay off your leveraged investment account at some point. So once your home equity line of credit is paid off, you'll stream $10,000 of that cash flow into a Tax Free Savings Account, (you're allowed to contribute up to $5,000 each year per person) and the balance into a high-interest savings account. This is where the extra $385,000 comes from in your cash account.

> Clearly, leveraging isn't an option for everyone. It is essential that you be able to comfortably service your debt payments. No investment strategy will be successful if it creates anxiety or financial hardship in your life.

"That way, even if market returns are poor, you won't have to break into your other accounts and risk selling when the markets are down when it comes time to pay the bank. And you can draw on this account for part of your income in your early retirement years. Not only will this give you more time to collect bonuses within your GMWB, but it will also give you a sense of security because you will truly have your rainy day account – without having to pay non-tax-deductible interest on the other side of your balance sheet."

I could see that Mel and Molly were both quietly delighted, but a little worn out.

"This is so much better than anything we've considered before," said Mel. "For the first time, I believe we will really be able to pay ourselves first. All the books say it, of course, but the way it works out is, pay the government and the bank first and then pray you have a bit left to save for your retirement. But your plan makes it possible."

WEIGHING THE RISKS

"There's no question we want to go ahead with this, Dessa," said Molly. "But I do have some questions. Like what happens to the plan if our leverage investment interest rates go up?"

"That's an important question, Molly. But there are two reasons I don't think it's something you should worry about. It has to do with the tax-deductibility of your interest. Take a look at these figures."

There are a lot of intense opinions - for and against - on the subject of using leverage to invest. Of course, everyone who has ever owned a home has used leverage, which is what makes owning a home possible and usually profitable.

If interest rates go up by one quarter of 1%, your monthly payment will increase by about $20 per month. However, we know that you're in a 46% tax bracket, so the net cost is only $11 per month. Rates would have to go up a lot before your payments would become unaffordable.

"Remember, too, that your monthly investment costs are lower than they were before, so you've got more wiggle room.

"The other reason I don't think you need to worry about rising interest rates is this: if interest rates are rising, it usually means that the economy is growing and the central bank may want to slow things down by raising rates. And when the economy is moving along well, so is the stock market. Remember, my worst case scenario is that we NEVER have any profits from markets, which is very unlikely. Finally, the interest rates we've used to calculate your plan are higher than today's rates."

> I have my own criteria regarding how much more great debt I may suggest a client take on. In addition to traditional debt ratios applied by lenders, several other issues need to be taken into account. A young doctor whose income is generally going up every year has a different ability to service debt than a salaried employee whose earning potential is capped at the rate of inflation.

"You've calculated your worst case scenario, Dessa, but my worst case scenario is a little different. What happens if I lose my job five years from now?" said Mel.

"Well, let's hope that never happens, Mel. But you're right to consider all the risks, and we know it happens, right? That's one of the benefits of working with a financial advisor. It's my job to consider provisions for all the 'what-ifs' so you have a lot less to keep you up at night," I said.

"Based on our plan, in five years, your total debt will be paid down to about $28,780, so your monthly interest will be reduced, too. Let's look at that compared to your current cash flow. Today you're paying $1,100 per month on your mortgage, then you will be paying about $100 in monthly interest. I guess what I'm trying to say is you will be a lot better off if you lose your job in five years with my plan than you would be without it."

"Okay, I get your point," said Mel.

"And don't forget that, in addition to being in a much better position in terms of cash flow, you will have also added an additional $50,000 to your RRSP, plus the increase in the monthly contributions, which add up to $45,000, and the added tax savings of $33,300. **In other words, there is nothing I can do to reduce the risk of you losing your job in five years, but with this plan, you will be $128,300 ahead and your payment obligations will be a lot less. That's where I'd want to be if I was looking at losing my job – with a much stronger balance sheet and greater net worth."**

> *Dessanomics* does more than help us save, it gives us freedom and peace of mind. We've been able to save enough for our boat, Derek's Harley and the family snowmobile. Give us a couple more years with this plan, and we'll have our dream cottage too!
>
> **THE CONSTRUCTION FOREMAN & THE POSTAL WORKER**

"Yeah, when you put it that way, there is no argument. Your plan is better," said Mel. "Whatever happens, if the markets are bad, or I lose my job, or I never get the same kind of overtime again, we're going to be alright. Better than alright. We're going to be golfing in Florida with Hank and Linda! And if something happens to either one of us, the other will be okay – and we'll both be okay if we live too long. You've got us covered on the downside and the upside. I'm liking it."

"I think Mel just said you were right, Dessa," said Molly, laughing and shaking her head. "In 30 years, I've only heard that a couple of times. Now I'm really impressed!"

"I feel so good about this," said Molly. "I never really knew how much I worried about all of this. I never knew if Mel had enough life insurance, if I'd be able to stay in our house if something happened, if we'd have enough money to retire on. I never really knew what a weight that was, but I just feel so much better knowing that you've covered all of this off. My only regret is that we didn't insist that Hank and Linda put us in touch with you five years ago."

"They did," said Mel, shaking his head. "But I thought we were on the right track. But hindsight is 20/20, right? I really like the idea that with the critical illness insurance we'll have, if one of us gets really sick, we'll be able to get the best care without derailing our retirement plan. That's something that's always worried me."

"I just can't wait until we have everything in place, Dessa," said Molly. "Where do we sign? I feel like we're unloading a truckload of stress I didn't even really know I had. And you know stress does terrible things to our health, not to mention our looks. Not only am I going to be able to afford to have a facial in the spa when we take our annual cruise on this plan, but I'm going to lose a lot of worry lines!"

"Yes, Molly," I said, unable to resist, "you will be forever Young."

Dessanomics KEY: 11

THE RISKS OF NOT USING LEVERAGE CAN BE FAR GREATER THAN THE RISKS OF USING LEVERAGE. THE KEY IS TO USE CONSERVATIVE LEVERAGE IN THE CONTEXT OF A SOLID OVERALL RETIREMENT PLAN.

Chapter 10:

AFTERWORD – GETTING THE ADVICE YOU NEED

■ ■ ■

If you're like most of the people who hear about the *Dessanomics* process, you'll want to put it to work in your life.

I encourage you to contact me or my team personally or find a financial advisor who's familiar with the process to help you put the plan in action. You can find a qualified professional in your area by visiting my website, www.askdessa.com. While it sounds pretty straightforward, and it is, it's essential that the plan be individualized to meet your specific personal needs.

For example, with Mel and Molly, I recommended borrowing to top up Mel's RRSP as soon as possible. Because of their specific income and tax situation, this worked well for them. However, that might not always be the case. If your income is lower, taking too much of a deduction in a single year may prevent you from getting the greatest refund benefit for your contribution. You will need professional advice to ensure you get the refund you deserve, and it may be best to spread your contribution over a series of years or even contribute to a non-registered account.

The same is true of the GMWB I recommended for the Youngs. While the principals of efficient cash flow apply to everyone, the specifics of the action plan depend on your individual needs and goals. The Youngs have no pension, no security in retirement, and that was a primary goal of our plan. They will have the upside of the market (albeit with a little less profit), with the downside protection of some guaranteed capital and guaranteed income. In the leveraged, non-registered account, they'll also have the most tax efficient investment available in the marketplace today.

Mel and Molly will also have liquidity, meaning that, if they need money for something else, they can always cash some or all of it out at market value. We've set up their plan in a way that ensures they'll never have to do that, but if for some reason their situation changed so dramatically that they wanted to do so, that option is available to them. A GMWB provides the growth and flexibility of a mutual fund, the protection of a GIC, and the guaranteed income stream of an annuity – everything in one tidy package.

That said, there is no single investment product that is a one-size-fits-all option for 100% of a portfolio. A professional advisor can help you define your retirement needs and design a diversified portfolio of products that meets all of them.

RRSPs are still our most efficient savings vehicles, providing a tax deduction now and the opportunity to compound tax-free, but it is important to consider all the options with your advisor. An experienced advisor can help you determine what blend of leverage, non-registered investments, TFSAs and registered investments will build your wealth most effectively.

If you're working with an advisor now, please don't be discouraged if he's initially resistant to this process. Advisors traditionally haven't paid as much attention to cash-flow efficiency as they have to the portfolio mix, and a significant shift in mind-set is required. But if they are committed professionals, once they've investigated the process and the new products in the marketplace (and read this book) I'm convinced they'll be sold. If not, once you've established their reasons for resistance, you may want to contact me or one of the advisors on our website.

Innovation isn't always welcomed with open arms, no matter how much of an improvement it represents. It's a funny thing. When Manulife offered the first GMWB to the Canadian market in late 2006, many in the media, and some advisors, felt that it was too expensive. Their view was that these types of guarantees were unnecessary for the average investor.

Now it's two years later. Manulife's Guaranteed Income Fund Select With Income Plus won an industry award for best new product. Several other firms have jumped on the bandwagon and Canadians have ploughed billions of dollars into these products. As luck would have it (good luck for those holding GMWBs and bad luck for those who sat on the sidelines), the Dow Jones Industrial Average is down 40%, and the experts who weighed in against guarantees have completely changed their tune. More importantly, the retired boomers who have GMWBs won't be returning to work because of market conditions.

My clients are delighted that we protected their investments. When stock markets are on the way up and the economy is strong, investors may not want to pay for protection. But at some point, they're going to be extremely grateful they have it, and it may be the one thing that keeps them from locking in their losses and derailing their retirement plan.

It is a financial advisor's responsibility to consider all aspects of a client's financial health. I have to admit that I think we've traditionally spent too much time on the investment aspect of the equation and too little time on critical matters such as efficient cash flow and peace of mind. That is slowly changing, and I hope we've demonstrated that what is good for peace of mind is also best for financial security.

Dessanomics

KEY: 12

GET THE HELP YOU DESERVE TO CREATE AN EFFICIENT RETIREMENT PLANNING SYSTEM. WHILE THIS PROCESS CAN HELP ANYONE WITH INCOME, IT'S ESSENTIAL THAT IT BE TAILORED TO YOUR INDIVIDUAL NEEDS.

Many books have been written on choosing the right asset mix. It's time, I think, to do more of what I've tried to do with this book – focus on having the correct products. But you can't use these tools until you change the way you run your cash flow machine.

Henry Ford was perhaps the most successful auto baron of all time. Revolutionizing automobile production by automating the assembly line, he made significant reductions in the amount of time and money it took to build a car. By doing so, he made the automobile affordable for the middle-class American, and the rest is history.

Similarly, Secretariat is known as perhaps the greatest racehorse of all time. After his death, an autopsy revealed that his heart was more than 2.5 times larger than that of an average thoroughbred. That great heart pumped more blood and oxygen, allowing him to run at higher speeds for a much longer time. That, of course, allowed Secretariat to win more races and set more records. Today, breeders try to produce thoroughbreds with larger hearts for greater efficiency.

You probably see where I'm going with this. In order to achieve success in any endeavour, you first have to create an efficient system. I don't know anyone who wouldn't like to save more money for retirement and provide more financial security for their families.

But until now, efficiency hasn't been a primary element of the plan, so the system simply didn't support success. *Dessanomics* takes the pay-yourself-first adage to an entirely new level and puts a secure, comfortable retirement within the reach of millions of Canadians. This combination of efficient cash flow with reduction of interest and income tax will propel you into a secure, comfortable retirement. It's the only process I know of that will.

> You now have all the keys.
> Unlock your wealth potential.

DESSANOMICS
WORKBOOK

■ ■ ■

Normally, when you get to this point in a book, it's the end. But with *Dessanomics* this is just the beginning! What's the best way to turn the knowledge you've gained into results? How can <u>you</u> master *Dessanomics?*

The answer is to commit yourself now – before you close the book. Do you remember what you learned about compounding? The sooner you get started, the closer you get to your million dollar difference. Or more!

Let's start by setting some goals.

Dessanomics

KEY:

13

TO BE HEALTHY IS SOMETHING YOU VALUE.
TO LOSE 10 LBS. IS A GOAL.

I've included a workbook page for you, and one for your spouse. In order for *Dessanomics* to be successful, you both need to complete this page and sign it – that's your commitment to yourselves and to the process.

*Instructions: Please complete all forms **before** your first meeting with your financial advisor.*

YOUR GOALS

I want to retire at age _____.

I want to have income of _____ per year.

I want to help my children _____.

I want to vacation at _____.

I want to spend more time _____.

I want to _____.

I want to _____.

_____

_____

_____
Your signature

_____
Your spouse as witness

*Instructions: Please complete all forms **before** your first meeting with your financial advisor.*

YOUR SPOUSE'S GOALS

I want to retire at age _____.

I want to have income of _____ per year.

I want to help my children _____.

I want to vacation at _____.

I want to spend more time _____.

I want to _____.

I want to _____.

_____

_____

_____
Your signature

_____
Your spouse as witness

YOUR BASIC PERSONAL INFORMATION

Name: _____

Address: _____

_____

Phone: _____

e-mail address: _____

Birthdate (mm/dd/yy): _____

Social Insurance No.: _____

ID (Birth Certificate or Driver's License): _____

_____

Occupation: _____

Employer: _____

YOUR SPOUSE'S BASIC PERSONAL INFORMATION

Name: _____

Address: _____

_____

Phone: _____

e-mail address: _____

Birthdate (mm/dd/yy): _____

Social Insurance No.: _____

ID (Birth Certificate or Driver's License): _____

_____

Occupation: _____

Employer: _____

FAMILY INFORMATION

First Child

Name: _____

Birthdate (mm/dd/yy): _____

Social Insurance No.: _____

Second Child

Name: _____

Birthdate (mm/dd/yy): _____

Social Insurance No.: _____

Third Child

Name: _____

Birthdate (mm/dd/yy): _____

Social Insurance No.: _____

Instructions: Please bring all of these documents to your first meeting with your financial advisor.

1. Current proof of income (you and your spouse).

2. Current and previous year tax returns and T-1 summary.

3. Current mortgage and loan statements (include auto, boat, and lines of credit and credit card statements).

4. Copies of (1) Life Insurance
        (2) Disability Insurance
        (3) Critical Illness Insurance
        (4) Long Term Care Insurance

5. Copy of Group Benefits from your employer.

6. Pension statements.

7. Statements for all investments.

8. Current bank balances.

9. Copy of auto lease.

For business owners:

1. Corporate tax returns (2 years).

2. Corporate financial statements (2 years).

LIST OF ASSETS

Cash - Bank Accounts - Chequing (1) _____

(2) _____

(3) _____

Savings (1) _____

(2) _____

Other _____

Life Insurance - Cash Value _____

Principal Residence (Market Value Home) (1) _____

Other real estate (2) _____

(3) _____

Automobiles (list only if you own them) (1) _____

(2) _____

(3) _____

(4) _____

ASSETS CONTINUED

Registered   (yours)   _____

(spouse)   _____

(children)   _____

Non-Registered   (yours)   _____

(spouse)   _____

(children)   _____

Other Assets   _____

e.g. Art/Antiques   _____

Total Assets   _____

LIABILITIES

(A) PERSONAL LOANS

	ISSUER	ORIGINAL AMOUNT	INTEREST RATE	PAYMENT/ MONTH	TERM	CURRENT BALANCE
(EXAMPLES)	ABC CREDIT UNION	$10,000	6.5%	$195/M	5 YRS.	$9,805
1.						
2.						
3.						

(A₁)TOTAL PAYMENTS _____ (A₂) TOTAL LOANS BALANCE _____

(B) MORTGAGE

	ISSUER	ORIGINAL AMOUNT	INTEREST RATE	PAYMENT/ MONTH	TERM	CURRENT BALANCE
1.						
2.						
3.						

(B₁)TOTAL PAYMENTS _____ (B₂) TOTAL LOANS BALANCE _____

(C) CREDIT CARDS

	ISSUER	INTEREST RATE	PAYMENT	CURRENT BALANCE
1.				
2.				
3.				
4.				
5.				
6.				
7.				
8.				

(C₁)TOTAL PAYMENTS _____ (C₂) TOTAL LOANS BALANCE _____

(D) AUTO/BOAT/TRAILER

ISSUER	ORIGINAL AMOUNT	INTEREST RATE	PAYMENT/ MONTH	TERM	CURRENT BALANCE
1.					
2.					
3.					
4.					
5.					

(D₁)TOTAL PAYMENTS _____ (D₂) TOTAL LOANS BALANCE _____

(E) OTHER

WHO	ORIGINAL AMOUNT	INTEREST RATE	PAYMENT/ MONTH	TERM	CURRENT BALANCE
1.					
2.					

(E₁)TOTAL PAYMENTS _____ (E₂) TOTAL LOANS BALANCE _____

TOTAL $(A_1) + (B_1) + (C_1) + (D_1) + (E_1) =$ TOTAL PAYMENTS _____

TOTAL $(A_2) + (B_2) + (C_2) + (D_2) + (E_2) =$ TOTAL LOANS BALANCE _____

YOUR PERSONAL CASH FLOW

ANNUAL INFLOWS

	TOTAL ANNUAL GROSS	COMMENTS
SALARY	$	
OVERTIME	$	
BONUS	$	
PENSION INCOME	$	
CPP INCOME	$	
OLD AGE SECURITY	$	
INTEREST INCOME	$	
DIVIDEND INCOME	$	
INVESTMENT INCOME	$	
RRSP INCOME	$	
RRIF INCOME	$	
OTHER INCOME	$	
TOTAL INFLOWS	$	
INCOME TAX	$	

ANNUAL DEDUCTIBLE EXPENSES

	TOTAL ANNUAL	COMMENTS
RSP CONTRIBUTIONS	$	
INVESTMENT EXPENSES	$	
CHILD CARE EXPENSES	$	
UNION/ASSOCIATION DUES	$	
CHARITABLE DONATIONS	$	
MEDICAL EXPENSES	$	
POLITICAL DONATIONS	$	
OTHER DEDUCTIBLES	$	
TOTAL DEDUCTIBLES	$	

YOUR SPOUSE'S PERSONAL CASH FLOW

ANNUAL INFLOWS

	TOTAL ANNUAL GROSS	COMMENTS
SALARY	$	
OVERTIME	$	
BONUS	$	
PENSION INCOME	$	
CPP INCOME	$	
OLD AGE SECURITY	$	
INTEREST INCOME	$	
DIVIDEND INCOME	$	
INVESTMENT INCOME	$	
RRSP INCOME	$	
RRIF INCOME	$	
OTHER INCOME	$	
TOTAL INFLOWS	$	
INCOME TAX	$	

ANNUAL DEDUCTIBLE EXPENSES

	TOTAL ANNUAL	COMMENTS
RSP CONTRIBUTIONS	$	
INVESTMENT EXPENSES	$	
CHILD CARE EXPENSES	$	
UNION/ASSOCIATION DUES	$	
CHARITABLE DONATIONS	$	
MEDICAL EXPENSES	$	
POLITICAL DONATIONS	$	
OTHER DEDUCTIBLES	$	
TOTAL DEDUCTIBLES	$	

MONTHLY LIFESTYLE EXPENSES

HOUSING	AMOUNT
PHONE/CELL	
ELECTRICITY	
GAS	
CABLE/INTERNET	
WATER/SEWER	
MAINTENANCE/REPAIRS	
SUPPLIES	
RENOVATIONS	
LAWN/YARD/POOL	
OTHER	
SUBTOTAL	

TRANSPORTATION	AMOUNT
LEASE PAYMENT	
LEASE PAYMENT (2)	
PUBLIC TRANSPORT	
INSURANCE	
LICENSING	
FUEL	
MAINTENANCE	
OTHER	
SUBTOTAL	

INSURANCE	AMOUNT
HOME	
HEALTH/DENTAL/DRUG	
LIFE	
OTHER	
SUBTOTAL	

ENTERTAINMENT	AMOUNT
VIDEO RENTALS	
MOVIES	
CONCERTS	
SPORTING EVENTS	
LIVE THEATRE	
OTHER	
OTHER	
OTHER	
SUBTOTAL	

TAXES	AMOUNT
PROPERTY	
OTHER	
SUBTOTAL	

RECREATION	AMOUNT
VACATION	
OTHER	
SUBTOTAL	

FOOD	AMOUNT
GROCERIES	
DINING OUT	
OTHER	
SUBTOTAL	

SUBSCRIPTIONS	AMOUNT
NEWSPAPER	
MAGAZINES	
SUBTOTAL	

PERSONAL CARE	AMOUNT
MEDICAL	
HAIR/NAILS	
CLOTHING	
DRY CLEANING	
HEALTH CLUB	
ORGANIZATION FEES	
OTHER	
SUBTOTAL	

PETS	AMOUNT
FOOD	
VETERINARY	
GROOMING	
TOYS	
OTHER	
SUBTOTAL	

GIFTS & CHARITY	AMOUNT
BIRTHDAY	
CHRISTMAS	
CHURCH	
CHARITY	
CHARITY	
SUBTOTAL	

LEGAL	AMOUNT
ATTORNEY	
CHILD SUPPORT	
ALIMONY	
OTHER	
SUBTOTAL	

TOTAL	

The wealthy hire financial advisors just like they hire lawyers and accountants – they don't go it alone and neither should you.

How to become one of my clients:

Contact:

Kaspardlov Laverty & Associates

1-877-974-4429

or

find a Dessanomics certified advisor
near you by going to
www.askdessa.com

ADVISORS & CORPORATE TRAINING

For training and certification

seminars in your area,

go to www.askdessa.com

or

call 1-877-974-4429